Betty Crocker's

OLD-FASHIONED

COOKBOOK

Betty Crocker's
OLD-FASHIONED COOKBOOK

PRENTICE HALL PRESS

New York ◆ London ◆ Toronto ◆ Sydney ◆ Tokyo ◆ Singapore

Illustrations courtesy of *Food and Drink: A Pictorial Archive from Nineteenth-Century Sources*. Selected by Jim Harter. Dover Publications, Inc., New York.

PRENTICE HALL PRESS
15 Columbus Circle
New York, NY 10023

Published simultaneously in Canada by Prentice Hall Canada, Inc.
PRENTICE HALL PRESS and colophons are registered trademarks
of Simon & Schuster Inc.

BETTY CROCKER is a registered trademark
of General Mills, Inc.

Library of Congress Cataloging-in-Publication Data

Crocker, Betty.
  [Old-fashioned cookbook]
  Betty Crocker's old-fashioned cookbook.—1st ed.
    p.   cm.
  ISBN 0-13-073693-7
  1. Cookery, American.   I. Title.
TX715.C92184   1990
641.5973—dc20   89-16404
                                                        CIP

Manufactured in the United States of America

10 9 8 7 6 5 4 3 2 1

First Edition

CONTENTS

Clockwise from upper right: Honey-baked Ham with Raisin Sauce (page 49), Squash Rolls (page 138), Plum Preserves (page 236), Country Apple Pie (page 168), Jelly Roll (page 185), Sweet-and-Sour Green Beans (page 86), Cherry Blinks (page 211), Whole Wheat Crackers (page 15), Watermelon Pickles (page 226), Pear-Apricot Chutney (page 235), Pepper Relish (page 231), Rhubarb-Strawberry Conserve (page 232), Cornmeal Biscuits (page 108), Ginger-glazed Carrots (page 88)

INTRODUCTION

The words *old-fashioned cooking* make us nostalgic for a time when family members gathered together around a table. Thoughts wander to the familiar foods that always comfort and inspire: warm-from-the-oven breads with golden crusts; steaming bowls of fragrant soups and stews; cookies and cakes for which adults are every bit as eager as children; homemade preserves that fill the house with rich fruit aroma while they simmer in the kettle and, packed into sparkling glass jars, glow in the light of the kitchen window like jewels.

These warming memories aren't fantasy; they are the solid foundation of heritage cookery, the kind of food that never goes out of style. Trends come and go, but the straightforward classics and family recipes handed from one generation to the next endure as our favorites. Old-fashioned cooking is simply the food we love best, yesterday, today and tomorrow.

Perhaps no figure better represents many of the virtues of old-fashioned cooking than Betty Crocker. Her reassuring role in the lives of American homemakers has made her a veritable institution for more than sixty-five years. When we were just growing accustomed to our ice boxes and gas-fired ovens, Betty Crocker was already standing by.

It all began in the early 1920s, when the Washburn-Crosby Company, now known as General Mills, hired its first home economist to test Gold Medal flour. In 1921, in a gesture to convey the company's philosophy of service, and in the belief that contact with homemakers should have a personal, feminine touch, Washburn-Crosby created Betty Crocker. (The name "Betty" was chosen because of its friendly sound; "Crocker" was the name of a retiring company director.)

In 1924, Betty Crocker was heard on the radio. Her "Cooking School on the Air" ran for twenty-four consecutive years, raising more than one generation of confident, creative cooks. Through the years, Betty Crocker and General Mills have responded to our changing needs in the kitchen. When the Depression crippled food budgets, recipes were developed to accommodate those more meager circumstances. When World War II led to food shortages and the rationing of butter, eggs and sugar, Gold Medal recipes again came to the rescue, making the most of what little was available.

Just as our great-grandmothers welcomed new conveniences, we too are constantly looking for ways to make cooking easier. In 1943, Gold Medal originated the one-bowl method of cake making, cutting mixing time in half. The brown-and-serve method for yeast-raised breads, developed in 1949, enabled the home baker to indulge in freshly baked breads at a moment's notice. And in 1961, the presifted flour introduced by Gold Medal eliminated still another baking step.

Perhaps you are fortunate enough to have been able to cook alongside your own grandmother, comfortably seated on a kitchen stool from where she could hand you the sifter and the rolling pin (dusted just so with flour) together with a good measure of advice. But whether you currently cook alone or with someone you love, *Betty Crocker's Old-Fashioned Cookbook* lets you enjoy the most cherished, delicious dishes from years gone by. Every recipe in this collection is a tried-and-true, old-fashioned classic. In some cases where older recipes called for excessive amounts of salt or fat, we have reduced those elements while remaining faithful to the essence of the traditional recipe. Some recipes even include alternative directions for using such modern conveniences as the electric mixer, food processor and the microwave.

We hope that you enjoy this extraordinary collection, with recipes from pre-Depression years to the glory days of the sock hop. Old-fashioned cooking keeps alive many of the traditions we hold dear and, more important, it means delicious recipes that simply can't be improved.

—The Betty Crocker Editors

Betty Crocker's
OLD-FASHIONED
COOKBOOK

Chapter 1

HORS D'OEUVRES AND CANAPÉS

*O*nly recently have meals in the Western world been scaled down to just a few courses, and for most of us that seems quite enough. For hundreds of years, people followed the fashion of setting as many dishes onto the table at one time as they could afford, and sweet dishes were served alongside meats, savory pies and the like. In the eighteenth century, "Russian service"—the consecutive serving of courses—began to grow in popularity. Our great-grandfathers were accustomed to meals that were complete "from soup to nuts," beginning with a clear broth or creamy bisque and concluding with nutmeats and perhaps a glass of port.

Today we live more simply, but we may never give up the tradition of starting our dinner (or luncheon) with an appetizing little preamble. Hors d'oeuvre is French for something "aside from the main effort," and originally it referred to a first course enjoyed at the table. With the advent of the cocktail in the 1920s and the "stand-up" cocktail party, people enjoyed hors d'oeuvres and canapés (tiny toasts with savory fillings and pretty garnishes) with their drinks, setting the style for entertaining for years to come.

Molded Salmon Spread (page 4) and Whole Wheat Crackers (page 15)

Molded Salmon Spread

2 cups boiling water
1 package (6 ounces) lemon-flavored gelatin
¾ cup cold water
½ cup dry white wine
1½ cups mayonnaise or salad dressing
¼ cup chopped green onions (with tops)
1 medium carrot, shredded
1 can (14¾ ounces) salmon, drained and finely
*   flaked*

Pour boiling water on gelatin in medium bowl; stir until gelatin is dissolved. Stir in cold water, wine and mayonnaise. Place bowl in bowl of ice and water, or refrigerate 20 to 30 minutes, stirring occasionally, just until mixture mounds slightly when dropped from a spoon. Stir in remaining ingredients. Pour into shallow 6-cup mold. Refrigerate about 2 hours or until firm. Unmold on serving plate. Garnish with fresh parsley if desired.

10 SERVINGS

Brandy Cheese Ball

4 ounces blue cheese, crumbled and softened
1 package (8 ounces) cream cheese, softened
½ to 1 clove garlic, finely chopped
2 tablespoons snipped fresh parsley
2 tablespoons brandy or Cognac
⅓ cup sesame seed, toasted

Beat blue cheese, cream cheese, garlic, parsley and brandy in small bowl on low speed until smooth. Cover and refrigerate about 6 hours or until firm.

Just before serving, shape cheese mixture into a ball; roll in sesame seed. Arrange fresh parsley or watercress around cheese ball if desired.

ABOUT **1½** CUPS

Chicken Liver Pâté

To prepare chicken livers, rinse them, pat them dry with paper toweling and snip out any loose membranes or veins. Since pâtés are classically baked in a crust, this dish could actually be referred to as a terrine.

8 ounces chicken livers
½ cup water
½ cup butter or margarine, softened
2 tablespoons finely chopped onion
1 teaspoon dry mustard
½ teaspoon salt
¼ teaspoon ground nutmeg
⅛ teaspoon ground cloves
⅛ teaspoon ground red pepper

Heat chicken livers and water to boiling in 1-quart saucepan; reduce heat. Cover and simmer 15 minutes; drain and cool. Place livers and remaining ingredients in blender container. Cover and blend on high speed about 1 minute, scraping sides occasionally, until smooth. Press in buttered 1-cup mold or glass bowl. Cover and refrigerate at least 3 hours but no longer than 2 days.

1 CUP

Microwave Directions. Cut chicken livers into 1-inch pieces; prick with fork. Place in 1½-quart microwavable casserole; add water. Cover tightly and microwave on medium (50%) 10 to 12 minutes, stirring after 5 minutes, until livers are no longer pink; drain and cool. Continue as directed.

Brandy Cheese Ball

Blue Cheese Dip

1 package (8 ounces) cream cheese, softened
4 ounces blue cheese, crumbled
1/3 cup sweet white wine
1 tablespoon snipped fresh parsley
1 teaspoon Worcestershire sauce
Dash of garlic powder
2 tablespoons snipped fresh parsley

Mix cream cheese and blue cheese in small bowl; stir in wine gradually. Beat until light and fluffy. Beat in 1 tablespoon parsley, the Worcestershire sauce and garlic powder. Cover and refrigerate until ready to serve. Garnish with 2 tablespoons parsley.

2 CUPS

Deviled Ham Dip

Like most deviled dishes, this one is zippy with the addition of mustard, Worcestershire sauce, onion and garlic. It's versatile, too: Once refrigerated, it firms up and doubles as a spread. Either way, it's *sinfully* delicious served with Whole Wheat Crackers (page 15).

1 package (8 ounces) cream cheese, softened
1 can (4 1/2 ounces) deviled ham
2 tablespoons dry red wine
3 tablespoons finely chopped dill pickle
2 tablespoons finely chopped onion
1 teaspoon Worcestershire sauce
1/4 teaspoon dry mustard
1 clove garlic, finely chopped

Beat cream cheese and deviled ham in small bowl until creamy; stir in wine gradually. Stir in remaining ingredients. Cover and refrigerate any remaining dip.

ABOUT 1 3/4 CUPS

Deviled Ham Spread. Cover and refrigerate about 8 hours or until firm.

Fruit with Honey Dip

Fifty years ago, this colorful tidbit would have been called a cocktail. If a ripe cantaloupe isn't available, 3 tart apples, sliced and dipped in pineapple juice, make a good substitute.

1 can (15 1/4 ounces) pineapple chunks in juice
Honey Dip (below)
2 bananas, cut into 1/2-inch slices
1 cantaloupe, scooped into balls or cut into
*   1-inch cubes*
1 pound seedless green grapes

Drain pineapple, reserving juice. Prepare Honey Dip. Toss banana slices in pineapple juice; drain. Arrange fruit on serving tray. Serve with Honey Dip.

10 SERVINGS

HONEY DIP

1 cup sour cream
1/2 cup mayonnaise or salad dressing
1/4 cup honey
1 tablespoon snipped fresh or 1 teaspoon
*   dried mint*
2 tablespoons reserved pineapple juice

Mix all ingredients; refrigerate.

Fruit with Honey Dip

Stuffed Cherry Tomatoes

Cherry tomatoes are bright, elegant additions to any appetizer tray. Colorful, easy to serve, and delicious with a variety of fillings, they're dainty enough to be eaten in one bite. A tiny slice cut from the bottom of each tomato keeps them steady on the platter.

1 pint cherry tomatoes (20 to 24 tomatoes)
1 package (8 ounces) cream cheese, softened
1 tablespoon plus 1 teaspoon milk
1 tablespoon prepared horseradish
1½ teaspoons snipped fresh or ½ teaspoon dried
dill weed
1 green onion (with top), finely chopped
Dill weed

Cut thin slice from stem ends of tomatoes. Remove pulp and seeds with melon baller or spoon; turn upside down on paper towel to drain. Mix cream cheese, milk, horseradish, 1½ teaspoons of the dill weed and the green onion. Fill tomatoes with cream cheese mixture; sprinkle with remaining dill weed. Cover and refrigerate until serving time.

8 SERVINGS

Open-Face Reuben Sandwiches

Serve this canapé-size version of the classic sandwich along with a variety of good, flavorful beers. Instead of chopping, use scissors to snip the sauerkraut and corned beef.

14 slices dark rye bread, toasted
Prepared mustard
1 can (16 ounces) sauerkraut, drained
and chopped
5 ounces (2 2.5-ounce packages) sliced
corned beef, finely chopped
2 cups shredded Swiss cheese (8 ounces)
½ cup mayonnaise or salad dressing

Heat oven to 375°. Spread toast lightly with mustard; place on ungreased cookie sheet. Mix sauerkraut, corned beef, cheese and mayonnaise. Spread about ⅓ cup sauerkraut mixture on each toast slice. Bake about 10 minutes or until sauerkraut mixture is hot and cheese is melted. Cut sandwiches into halves.

28 SANDWICHES

Party Sandwiches

PARTY SANDWICH BASES

Remove crusts from 8 slices firm white or wheat sandwich bread. Cut each slice into 4 squares or triangles. Spread with 1 of the following Spreads. Top with 1 or 2 of the Toppings.

32 SANDWICH BASES

SPREADS

* 1 container (8 ounces) soft cream cheese
* 2 packages (3 ounces each) cream cheese, softened, mixed with 2 teaspoons prepared horseradish
* 2 packages (3 ounces each) cream cheese, softened, mixed with 1½ teaspoons snipped fresh or ½ teaspoon dried dill weed
* ⅓ cup butter or margarine, softened, mixed with 1 tablespoon sliced green onion (with top)
* ⅓ cup butter or margarine, softened, mixed with 1 tablespoon snipped fresh parsley
* ⅓ cup mayonnaise or salad dressing mixed with 1 tablespoon grated onion

TOPPINGS

* finely chopped hard-cooked eggs
* thinly sliced cucumber
* sliced ripe or pimiento-stuffed olives
* pickle fan (For each fan, cut a ½-inch slice of tiny sweet pickle. Make 4 lengthwise cuts almost to the end of each piece. Spread gently to form a fan.)
* chopped nuts
* cooked tiny shrimp
* sliced cherry tomatoes
* sliced green onions (with tops)
* smoked oysters
* tiny pearl onions
* capers
* chopped pimiento

Onion-Cheese Puffs

1 cup water
⅓ cup butter or margarine
1 cup all-purpose flour
1 teaspoon salt
¼ teaspoon garlic powder
4 eggs
¾ cup shredded Swiss cheese (6 ounces)
1 small onion, chopped (about ¼ cup)

Heat oven to 400°. Heat water and butter to rolling boil in medium saucepan. Stir in flour, salt and garlic powder. Stir vigorously over low heat about 1 minute or until mixture forms a ball; remove from heat. Beat in eggs, all at once, until smooth. Stir in cheese and onion.

Drop dough by scant teaspoonfuls about 1 inch apart onto lightly greased cookie sheet. Bake 20 to 25 minutes or until puffed and golden; cool.

ABOUT 6 DOZEN PUFFS

Filled Puffs. Place 1 salted peanut, ½-inch fully cooked smoked ham cube or half of 1 pimiento-stuffed olive on each puff. Top with enough dough to cover. Bake as directed.

Topped Puffs. Place 1 pimiento-stuffed olive or ½-inch-square cheese slice (⅛ inch thick) on each puff. Bake as directed.

Prunes in Bacon

The contrast of salty and sweet lends excitement to this simple hors d'oeuvre. Use plump, moist prunes for the best results.

12 slices bacon (about 10 ounces)
24 large pitted prunes (about 9 ounces)

Heat oven to 400°. Cut bacon slices into halves. Wrap each half-slice bacon around 1 prune; secure with wooden pick. Place on rack in broiler pan. Bake about 20 minutes, without turning, until bacon is crisp.

8 SERVINGS

Whole Wheat Crackers

Yes, you can make crackers at home! To give them their characteristic "crack," thinly roll out the dough and bake on ungreased cookie sheets.

1½ cups all-purpose flour
1½ cups whole wheat flour
1 tablespoon sugar
1¼ teaspoons baking soda
1 teaspoon salt
1 cup buttermilk
¼ cup vegetable oil
Butter or margarine, melted

Heat oven to 350°. Mix flours, sugar, baking soda and salt. Stir in buttermilk and oil. Shape dough into 6 balls. Roll each ball into 9-inch square on lightly floured cloth-covered board. Cut into 2¼-inch squares; brush with butter. Place squares on ungreased cookie sheet. Sprinkle with coarse salt or sesame or poppy seed if desired. Bake 8 to 10 minutes or until crisp and golden.

ABOUT 8 DOZEN CRACKERS

Chapter 2

POULTRY, FISH AND SHELLFISH

*C*hicken at Sunday dinner was indeed a treat, since hens were valu-able egg layers, saved for such special occasions as celebrating guests. Heritage recipes for chicken reflect the care and enthusiasm that went into preparing a special dish, often using thick, yellow cream, marvelous spices and sprightly fresh herbs. The chicken that scratched out her life in a turn-of-the-century barnyard was scrawnier than her plump sisters today, but there was something to say for the flavor of a bird that spent its day strutting free under a blue sky.

Raising chickens may not have been troublesome, but preparing them for the pot was quite a chore. Here is advice from the **Washburn-Crosby Co. Gold Medal Flour Cook Book,** published in 1910: "To Dress and Clean Poultry: Pick off pin feathers, singe to remove hairs, cut the skin of neck near the head, push skin back and disjoint head at base of neck." Many intermediate steps follow, concluding with this instruction: "Wipe inside and outside, looking carefully to see that everything has been removed."

By the end of the nineteenth century, shellfish had begun to lose its reputation as cheap food for the masses, and fashionable French prepara-tions appeared in fancy American restaurants. Because the American colonies were coastal, we have a long-lived love of seafood. Not everyone lives near a fishmonger, but because most frozen seafood is packed in ice immediately after being hauled into the fish boat, we are virtually assured freshness and excellent quality.

Roast Turkey with Oyster Stuffing (page 18)

Roast Turkey with Oyster Stuffing

Few of us can imagine Thanksgiving without roast turkey, complete with all the trimmings. And each holiday season brings on new debates: What is the perfect way to prepare the bird? What stuffing should be used? And who gets to snap the wishbone?

Oyster stuffing is a classic preparation that dates back to eighteenth-century Maryland, when oysters were so plentiful and cheap that they were given away free at Baltimore bars. Years ago, the saying went, "Eat oysters only in months spelled with the letter R." Today, thanks to modern refrigeration, oysters are available and tasty all year round. Nonetheless, they're still at their sweet, succulent best during the cooler months, making this ideal Thanksgiving fare.

½ cup butter or margarine
1 cup chopped celery
1 cup chopped leeks (with tops)
9 cups soft bread cubes
1 pint shucked oysters, rinsed, drained and chopped (reserve liquid)*
1 cup snipped fresh parsley
1½ teaspoons fresh snipped or ½ teaspoon dried marjoram
1 teaspoon salt
½ teaspoon pepper
10- to 12-pound turkey
Butter or margarine, melted

Heat ½ cup butter in Dutch oven over medium heat until melted. Cook and stir celery and leeks in butter until tender; remove from heat. Stir in remaining ingredients except turkey and melted butter. Stir in enough reserved oyster liquid, if necessary, to moisten stuffing.

Heat oven to 325°. Fill wishbone area of turkey lightly with stuffing. Fasten neck skin to back with skewers. Fold wings across back with tips touching. Fill body cavity lightly. (Do not pack—stuffing will expand while cooking.) Tuck drumsticks under band of skin at tail, or tie or skewer to tail. Spoon remaining stuffing into small greased casserole; cover and refrigerate. Place in oven with turkey during last 30 minutes of roasting.

Place turkey, breast side up, on rack in shallow roasting pan. Brush with melted butter. Insert meat thermometer so tip is in thickest part of inside thigh muscle or thickest part of breast meat and does not touch bone. Roast uncovered 3½ to 4 hours or until thermometer registers 185°. Brush turkey with pan drippings 2 or 3 times during roasting. Place a tent of aluminum foil loosely over turkey when it begins to turn golden. After 2½ hours, cut band or remove skewer holding legs. Let stand about 20 minutes for easiest carving.

As soon as possible after serving, remove every bit of stuffing from turkey. Cool stuffing and turkey meat promptly; refrigerate separately. Use stuffing within 1 or 2 days and turkey meat within 2 or 3 days. Turkey meat can be frozen up to 3 weeks.

14 TO 16 SERVINGS

*2 cans (8 ounces each) oysters can be substituted for the shucked oysters.

Duck with Fruit Stuffing

Fruit's sweet and tangy flavor is the perfect foil for rich duck. This dried fruit stuffing is reminiscent of Scandinavian preparations for poultry.

3 cups dry bread cubes
1 cup cut-up prunes
½ cup cut-up dried apricots
¼ cup chopped onion
1 teaspoon grated orange peel
¼ cup orange juice
2 tablespoons butter or margarine, melted
1 teaspoon salt
½ teaspoon ground nutmeg
¼ teaspoon ground mace
1 egg, beaten
4- to 5-pound duckling

Heat oven to 350°. Mix all ingredients except duckling in large bowl. Fill wishbone area of duckling lightly with stuffing. Fasten neck skin to back with skewers. Fold wings across back with tips touching. Fill body cavity lightly. (Do not pack—stuffing will expand while cooking.) Fasten opening with skewers. Spoon remaining stuffing into small greased baking dish; cover and refrigerate. Place in oven with duckling during last 30 minutes of roasting.

Place duckling, breast side up, on rack in shallow roasting pan. Prick skin with fork. Roast uncovered about 3 hours or until drumstick meat feels very soft when pressed between fingers (remove excess fat from pan occasionally). Place a tent of aluminum foil loosely over duckling when it begins to turn golden. Let stand 10 minutes for easiest carving.

4 SERVINGS

Fried Chicken with Gravy

2½- to 3-pound broiler-fryer chicken, cut up
½ cup all-purpose flour
1 teaspoon salt
½ teaspoon paprika
¼ teaspoon pepper
Vegetable oil
Gravy (below)

Remove any excess fat from chicken. Mix flour, salt, paprika and pepper. Coat chicken with flour mixture. Heat oil (¼ inch) in 10- or 12-inch skillet until hot. Cook chicken in oil over medium heat 15 to 20 minutes or until light brown; reduce heat. Cover tightly and simmer 30 to 40 minutes, turning once or twice, until thickest pieces are done. If skillet cannot be covered tightly, add 1 to 2 tablespoons water. Remove cover during last 5 minutes of cooking to crisp chicken. Serve with Gravy.

4 SERVINGS

GRAVY

¼ cup drippings (fat and juices)
¼ cup all-purpose flour
1 cup liquid (meat juices, broth, water)
1 cup milk
Salt and pepper to taste

Pour drippings from skillet into bowl, leaving brown particles in skillet. Return ¼ cup drippings to skillet. Stir in flour. Cook over low heat, stirring constantly, until mixture is smooth and bubbly; remove from heat. Stir in liquid and milk. Heat to boiling, stirring constantly. Boil and stir 1 minute. Stir in salt and pepper.

Barbecued Chicken

Sometimes, it's just not possible to get out the grill for a real barbecue. This tangy, tomato-based sauce imparts barbecue flavor to baked chicken—without all those messy coals!

½ cup all-purpose flour
1 teaspoon salt
1 teaspoon paprika
¼ teaspoon pepper
2½- to 3-pound broiler-fryer chicken, cut up
¼ cup butter or margarine
Barbecue Sauce (below)

Heat oven to 425°. Remove any excess fat from chicken. Mix flour, salt, paprika and pepper. Coat chicken with flour mixture. Heat butter in rectangular baking dish, 13 × 9 × 2 inches, in oven until melted. Place chicken pieces, skin sides down, in dish. Bake 45 minutes; drain fat from dish and turn chicken. Reduce oven temperature to 375°. Spoon hot Barbecue Sauce over chicken. Bake 15 minutes or until thickest pieces are done.

4 TO 6 SERVINGS

BARBECUE SAUCE

1 cup ketchup or 1 can (8 ounces) tomato sauce
½ cup hot water
⅓ cup lemon juice
1 teaspoon salt
1 teaspoon sugar
2 teaspoons paprika
½ teaspoon pepper
1 tablespoon Worcestershire sauce
1 medium onion, finely chopped (about ½ cup)

Heat all ingredients to boiling, stirring occasionally.

Brown Chicken Fricassee

The name "fricassee" refers to any simmered meat, sautéed a little, a lot or not at all before the liquid is added. White fricassees call for very brief sautéing to keep the gravy light and delicate. Brown fricassees derive their deep color and more pronounced flavor from longer sautéing. Plan on serving lots of fluffy mashed potatoes or cooked rice to soak up every last bit of the mushroom-rich gravy.

3- to 3½-pound broiler-fryer chicken, cut up
1 cup all-purpose flour
1 teaspoon salt
¼ teaspoon pepper
2 tablespoons vegetable oil
2 cups water
1 cup sliced mushrooms
1 medium onion, chopped (about ½ cup)
2 bay leaves
2 tablespoons all-purpose flour
½ teaspoon salt
3 tablespoons water

Remove any excess fat from chicken. Mix 1 cup flour, 1 teaspoon salt and the pepper. Coat chicken with flour mixture. Heat oil in Dutch oven or 12-inch skillet until hot. Cook chicken in oil over medium-high heat 20 to 25 minutes or until brown. Add 2 cups water, the mushrooms, onion and bay leaves. Cover and cook over low heat 45 to 60 minutes or until thickest pieces of chicken are done.

Remove chicken; keep warm. Mix 2 tablespoons flour, ½ teaspoon salt and 3 tablespoons water in small bowl until smooth; stir into hot liquid. Heat to boiling, stirring constantly. Boil and stir 1 minute; reduce heat. Return chicken to Dutch oven. Cover and simmer 5 minutes. Remove bay leaves. Serve chicken over hot mashed potatoes or cooked rice if desired.

6 SERVINGS

Barbecued Chicken

Chicken Cacciatore

3- to 3½-pound broiler-fryer chicken, cut up
¼ cup shortening
½ cup all-purpose flour
1 medium green bell pepper
2 medium onions
2 cloves garlic, crushed
1 can (16 ounces) whole tomatoes, drained
1 can (8 ounces) tomato sauce
1 can (4 ounces) sliced mushrooms, drained
½ teaspoon salt
*1½ teaspoons snipped fresh or ½ teaspoon
    dried oregano*
*1 teaspoon snipped fresh or ¼ teaspoon
    dried basil*
Grated Parmesan cheese

Remove any excess fat from chicken. Heat shortening in 12-inch skillet until melted. Coat chicken with flour. Cook chicken in shortening over medium-high heat 15 to 20 minutes or until brown; drain on paper towels.

Cut bell pepper and onions crosswise into halves; cut each half into fourths. Stir bell pepper, onions and remaining ingredients except Parmesan cheese into skillet. Cover and simmer 30 to 40 minutes or until thickest pieces of chicken are done. Serve with Parmesan cheese.

6 SERVINGS

Chicken Pot Pie

3 tablespoons butter or margarine
3 tablespoons all-purpose flour
½ teaspoon salt
*1 teaspoon snipped fresh or ¼ teaspoon
    dried thyme*
⅛ teaspoon pepper
¾ cup chicken broth
¾ cup whipping cream
*2 cups cooked chicken or turkey, cut into
    1-inch pieces*
1 package (10 ounces) frozen peas and carrots*
1 cup frozen or canned small whole onions
Pastry for 9-inch Two-Crust Pie (page 166)

Heat butter in 3-quart saucepan over low heat until melted. Stir in flour, salt, thyme and pepper. Cook, stirring constantly, until mixture is smooth and bubbly; remove from heat. Stir in broth and whipping cream. Heat to boiling, stirring constantly. Boil and stir 1 minute. Stir in chicken, peas and carrots and onions.

Heat oven to 425°. Prepare pastry. Roll ⅔ of the pastry into 12-inch square; fit into square baking dish, 8 × 8 × 2 inches. Pour chicken mixture into pastry-lined dish. Roll remaining pastry into rectangle, about 10 × 6 inches. Cut rectangle into 12 strips, each ½ inch wide.

Place 7 pastry strips across filling; arrange remaining strips crisscross to make lattice top. Trim; turn edge of bottom crust over strips. Seal and flute. Bake 35 to 40 minutes or until light brown.

6 SERVINGS

*1 can (16 ounces) peas and carrots, drained, can be substituted for the frozen peas and carrots.

Poached Salmon with Hollandaise Sauce

Hollandaise Sauce (below)
3 cups water
1 teaspoon salt
4 black peppercorns
3 lemon slices
3 sprigs fresh parsley
1 small onion, sliced
1 bay leaf
4 salmon steaks, 1 inch thick (2 pounds)

Prepare Hollandaise Sauce. Heat water, salt, peppercorns, lemon slices, parsley, onion and bay leaf to boiling in 12-inch skillet; reduce heat. Cover and simmer 5 minutes. Place salmon steaks in skillet; add water, if necessary, to cover. Heat to boiling; reduce heat. Simmer uncovered 12 to 15 minutes or until fish flakes easily with fork. Serve with Hollandaise Sauce.

4 SERVINGS

HOLLANDAISE SAUCE

3 egg yolks
1 tablespoon lemon juice
½ cup firm butter*

Stir egg yolks and lemon juice vigorously in 1½-quart saucepan. Add ¼ cup of the butter. Stir over very low heat, stirring constantly, until butter is melted. Add remaining butter. Continue stirring vigorously until butter is melted and sauce is thickened. (Be sure butter melts slowly as this gives eggs time to cook and thicken sauce without curdling.) Serve hot or at room temperature. Cover and refrigerate any remaining sauce; to serve, stir in small amount of hot water.

*Do not use margarine in this recipe.

Fillet of Sole with Tartar Sauce

Tartar Sauce (below)
1 pound sole fillets, cut into serving pieces
½ teaspoon salt
Dash of pepper
2 tablespoons butter or margarine, melted
1 tablespoon lemon juice
1 teaspoon finely chopped onion

Heat oven to 400°. Prepare Tartar Sauce. Arrange sole fillets in ungreased square baking dish, 8 × 8 × 2 inches; sprinkle with salt and pepper. Mix butter, lemon juice and onion; drizzle over fish. Bake uncovered 25 to 30 minutes or until fish flakes easily with fork. Serve with Tartar Sauce.

4 SERVINGS

TARTAR SAUCE

1 cup mayonnaise or salad dressing
2 tablespoons finely chopped dill pickle
1 tablespoon snipped fresh parsley
2 teaspoons chopped pimiento
1 teaspoon grated onion

Mix all ingredients; cover and refrigerate.

Microwave Directions. Sprinkle sole fillets with salt and pepper. Fold in half; arrange in circle with folded sides to outside edge in ungreased microwavable pie plate, 9 × 1¼ inches. Mix butter, lemon juice and onion; drizzle over fish. Cover tightly and microwave on high 4 to 7 minutes, rotating pie plate ½ turn after 2 minutes, until fish flakes easily with fork.

Fish Timbales with Curry Sauce

2 tablespoons butter or margarine
¼ cup chopped onion
1 pound halibut or cod fillets, cut into
*   1-inch pieces*
1 cup milk
½ cup dry bread crumbs
½ teaspoon salt
¼ teaspoon ground nutmeg
⅛ teaspoon pepper
3 eggs
Curry Sauce (below)

Heat oven to 350°. Grease six 6-ounce custard cups. Heat butter in 10-inch skillet over medium heat until melted. Cook onion in butter until tender. Add halibut pieces and milk. Heat to simmering (do not boil); reduce heat. Cover and simmer 5 minutes or until fish flakes easily with fork. Place mixture in food processor work bowl or blender container. Cover and process on high speed about 1 minute, stopping blender occasionally to scrape sides, until smooth.

Mix fish mixture, bread crumbs, salt, nutmeg, pepper and eggs. Pour into custard cups. Place cups in rectangular pan, 13 × 9 × 2 inches, on oven rack. Pour very hot water into pan to within ½ inch of tops of cups. Bake 30 minutes or until knife inserted in center comes out clean. Unmold and serve with Curry Sauce.

6 SERVINGS

CURRY SAUCE

1 tablespoon butter or margarine
1 tablespoon all-purpose flour
½ teaspoon curry powder
¼ teaspoon salt
⅛ teaspoon pepper
1 cup milk

Heat butter in 1½-quart saucepan over low heat until melted. Stir in flour, curry powder, salt and pepper. Cook over low heat, stirring constantly, until smooth and bubbly; remove from heat. Stir in milk. Heat to boiling, stirring constantly. Boil and stir 1 minute.

Codfish Cakes

Salt cod was standard winter fare for early New Englanders, who preserved vast quantities of fish in salt to see them through the cold months. Most Pilgrim households counted a barrel of salt cod among their staples. Even after soaking in water, a little salt cod goes a long way.

4 ounces boneless salt cod
5 or 6 medium potatoes, pared and cut into
*   ½-inch cubes (about 5 cups)*
⅓ cup finely chopped onion
2 tablespoons all-purpose flour
⅛ teaspoon pepper
Vegetable oil
Ketchup

Place cod in bowl; cover with cold water. Cover and refrigerate 2 hours to remove excess salt; drain.

Cut cod into about ½-inch pieces. Place cod, potatoes and onion in 3-quart saucepan; cover with hot water. Heat to boiling. Cover and cook about 10 minutes or until potatoes are tender; drain. Beat cod mixture in large bowl about 1 minute on high speed until smooth. Stir in flour and pepper. Refrigerate about 1 hour or until cool.

Heat oil (1 to 1½ inches) in Dutch oven to 375°. Drop cod mixture by rounded tablespoonfuls, 4 or 5 at a time, into hot oil. Fry about 2 minutes or until golden brown; drain on paper towels. Serve with ketchup.

6 SERVINGS

Deviled Crabs

This recipe tucks gently seasoned crabmeat back into the crab shells for an elegant first course presentation. If you don't have crab shells, scallop shells or even ramekins are suitable substitutions.

>1 cup soft bread crumbs (about 2 slices bread)
>1/4 cup milk
>2 cups flaked crabmeat*
>1/4 cup butter or margarine, melted
>1/2 teaspoon dry mustard
>1/8 teaspoon ground red pepper
>1 egg, beaten
>1 green onion (with top), chopped

Heat oven to 400°. Grease 6 of the largest crab shells or 6-ounce ramekins. Mix bread crumbs and milk in large bowl. Mix in remaining ingredients gently. Spoon into shells. Place shells in jelly roll pan, 15½ × 10½ × 1 inch. Bake 20 to 25 minutes or until light brown.

6 SERVINGS

Boiled Hard-Shell Crabs (below) or 2 packages (6 ounces each) frozen crabmeat, thawed, drained and cartilage removed, can be used.

BOILED HARD-SHELL CRABS

>3 quarts water
>12 live or frozen (thawed) hard-shell blue crabs

Heat water to boiling in Dutch oven. Drop 6 crabs into Dutch oven. Cover and heat to boiling; reduce heat. Simmer 10 minutes; drain. Repeat with remaining 6 crabs. To remove meat, grasp body of crab. Break off large claws; remove meat from claws carefully. Pull off top shell; reserve. Cut or break off legs. Scrape off the gills; remove organs located in center part of body carefully. Remove meat from body. Scrub reserved shells with vegetable brush before filling.

Shrimp Boiled in Beer

Tasty? Yes. Neat? Absolutely not! So roll up your sleeves, tie on the bibs, and line the table with newspapers. Place the shrimp in a big bowl in the middle of the table. Then dig in! Be sure to pass lots of beer—and paper napkins.

>Cocktail Sauce (below)
>4 cans or bottles (12 ounces each) beer (room temperature) or 1½ quarts water
>1 tablespoon salt
>3 pounds fresh or frozen raw medium shrimp (in shells)

Prepare Cocktail Sauce. Heat beer and salt to boiling in Dutch oven; add shrimp. Heat just to boiling; reduce heat. Cover and simmer 3 to 5 minutes or until shrimp are pink; drain. Serve with Cocktail Sauce or, if desired, melted butter or margarine. (Provide containers for the discarded shells.)

4 OR 5 SERVINGS

COCKTAIL SAUCE

>1/2 cup ketchup
>2 tablespoons lemon juice
>2 to 3 teaspoons prepared horseradish

Mix all ingredients.

Microwave Directions. Reduce beer to 12 ounces. Mix ½ cup beer and ¼ teaspoon salt in microwavable pie plate, 10 × 1½ inches. Arrange 1 pound shrimp in pie plate. Cover tightly and microwave on high 5 to 6 minutes or until shrimp turn pink. Repeat with remaining shrimp.

Deviled Crabs

Jambalaya

This Southern one-pot dish needs only a salad and bread to round out the meal. "Jambalaya" comes from *jambon*, French for "ham," traditionally included. Be sure to watch the shrimp, both during the initial cooking and after adding them to the rice, to prevent overcooking.

2 medium onions, chopped
½ medium green bell pepper, chopped
1 clove garlic, finely chopped
3 tablespoons olive or vegetable oil
1 pound fresh or frozen raw shrimp, peeled
*   and deveined*
1 cup uncooked regular rice
2 cups chicken broth
1 can (16 ounces) tomatoes, undrained
1 teaspoon salt
⅛ teaspoon pepper
⅛ teaspoon ground thyme
⅛ teaspoon red pepper sauce
1 bay leaf
½ pound cubed cooked ham (about 1½ cups)

Cook and stir onions, bell pepper, garlic and 2 tablespoons of the oil in Dutch oven over low heat 3 minutes; add shrimp. Cook about 5 minutes, stirring frequently, until shrimp are pink. Remove shrimp mixture; reserve.

Cook remaining 1 tablespoon oil and the rice in Dutch oven over medium-high heat about 10 minutes, stirring frequently, until rice is light brown. Stir in broth, tomatoes, salt, pepper, thyme, pepper sauce and bay leaf. Heat to boiling; reduce heat. Cover and simmer about 15 minutes or until rice is tender. Stir in reserved shrimp mixture and the ham. Cover and cook just until shrimp and ham are hot. Remove bay leaf.

6 SERVINGS

Fried Clams

Vegetable oil
½ cup all-purpose flour
1 teaspoon salt
¼ teaspoon pepper
1 pint shucked clams (about 3½ dozen
*   in the shell)*
3 eggs, beaten
1½ cups dry bread crumbs

Heat oil (1 to 1½ inches) in Dutch oven to 375°. Mix flour, salt and pepper. Cut large clams in half. Coat clams with flour mixture; dip into eggs, then coat with bread crumbs. Fry 1 to 2 minutes or until golden brown; drain on paper towels.

6 SERVINGS

Fried Clams and Mixed Bean Salad (page 105)

Seafood Ragout in Puff Pastry Shells

1 package (10 ounces) frozen patty shells

2 tablespoons butter or margarine

8 ounces mushrooms, sliced

1 tablespoon snipped fresh parsley

1 green onion (with top), chopped

2 tablespoons all-purpose flour

½ teaspoon salt

⅛ teaspoon white pepper

⅛ teaspoon ground nutmeg

1½ cups milk

8 ounces sole or flounder fillets, cut into
    1-inch pieces

8 ounces fresh or frozen raw shrimp, peeled
    and deveined

8 ounces scallops*

1 cup sour cream

1 to 2 tablespoons sherry

Prepare pasty shells as directed on package. Heat butter in 3-quart saucepan until melted. Cook and stir mushrooms, parsley and onion in butter over low heat 5 minutes. Stir in flour, salt, white pepper and nutmeg. Cook over low heat, stirring constantly, until mixture is bubbly; remove from heat. Stir in milk. Heat to boiling, stirring constantly. Boil and stir 1 minute. Stir in sole pieces, shrimp and scallops. Cover and cook 3 to 5 minutes or until fish flakes easily with fork and shrimp are pink. Stir in sour cream and sherry; heat through. Serve in patty shells.

6 SERVINGS

If scallops are large, cut into quarters.

Seafood Ragout in Puff Pastry Shells

Chapter 3

BEEF, VEAL, PORK AND LAMB

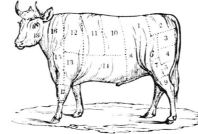

*W*hat was true one hundred years ago is true today: Let your wallet and your waistline determine the cuts of meat you prepare most often. Frequently, lean cuts are less expensive. Our grandmothers knew how to make the most of economical cuts, braising, stewing or simmering them to make them their tender best. Pot roasts and such stews as Burgundy Beef and heavenly Veal Daube come to the table with the savor of unhurried cooking, their rich sauces smothering egg noodles or hot potatoes.

In the pages that follow are the roasts we dream of when we're ravenous: Roast Beef with Yorkshire Pudding, Roast Pork Loin with Yam-stuffed Apples and Minted Leg of Lamb. Comforting, warming dishes, too: Scalloped Potatoes and Ham, Meatloaf and even Red Flannel Hash, virtually unchanged since the early years of this nation. These are the dishes that sent us with contented smiles to our childhood beds and sustained us as we trudged through drifts of snow on the way to school.

Herbed Pot Roast with Vegetables (page 36) and Mashed Potatoes (page 73)

Broiled Flank Steak

1½- to 2-pound beef flank steak or round steak
1½ teaspoons snipped fresh or ½ teaspoon
dried oregano
1 teaspoon salt
½ teaspoon celery seed
½ teaspoon pepper
2 tablespoons lemon juice
1 clove garlic, finely chopped

Score both sides of beef steak in diamond pattern ¼ inch deep. Mix remaining ingredients; rub into beef. Place in plastic bag or shallow glass dish. Fasten bag securely or cover dish with plastic wrap. Refrigerate at least 5 hours.

Set oven control to broil. Broil beef with top 2 to 3 inches from heat about 5 minutes or until brown. Turn; broil 5 minutes or until beef is desired doneness.

6 TO 8 SERVINGS

Beef Stroganoff

This elegant entrée, named for a wealthy merchant family in St. Petersburg (now Leningrad), combines a classic Russian sour cream sauce with top-quality beef, onions and mushrooms. Don't let the sauce boil once you've added the sour cream or it will curdle.

2 pounds beef sirloin steak, ½ inch thick
8 ounces mushrooms, sliced
2 medium onions, thinly sliced
1 clove garlic, finely chopped
¼ cup butter or margarine
1½ cups beef broth
½ teaspoon salt
1 teaspoon Worcestershire sauce
¼ cup all-purpose flour
1½ cups sour cream
4 cups hot cooked egg noodles

Cut beef steak across grain into strips, 1½ × ½ inch. Cook and stir mushrooms, onions and garlic in butter in 10-inch skillet until onions are tender; remove from skillet. Cook beef in same skillet until brown. Stir in 1 cup of the broth, the salt and Worcestershire sauce. Heat to boiling; reduce heat. Cover and simmer 15 minutes. Stir remaining ½ cup broth into flour; stir into beef mixture. Add onion mixture; heat to boiling, stirring constantly. Boil and stir 1 minute. Stir in sour cream; heat until hot (do not boil). Serve over noodles.

8 SERVINGS

Broiled Flank Steak, Corn Custard (page 88) and Coleslaw (page 103)

Burgundy Beef

4 pounds beef round steak, 1 inch thick
¼ cup shortening or bacon fat
5 large onions, sliced
1 pound mushrooms, sliced
3 tablespoons all-purpose flour
2 teaspoons salt
1 teaspoon snipped fresh or ¼ teaspoon
dried marjoram
1 teaspoon snipped fresh or ¼ teaspoon
dried thyme
¼ teaspoon pepper
1 cup beef broth
2 cups red Burgundy or other dry red wine

Cut beef steak into 1-inch cubes. Heat shortening in Dutch oven until melted. Cook beef in shortening over medium heat until brown and liquid has evaporated; remove. Cook and stir onions and mushrooms in Dutch oven until onions are tender, adding shortening if necessary. Remove mushrooms and onions; cover and refrigerate.

Return beef to Dutch oven; sprinkle with flour, salt, marjoram, thyme and pepper. Stir in broth and Burgundy. Heat to boiling; reduce heat. Cover and simmer about 1¼ hours or until beef is tender. (Liquid should just cover beef.) If necessary, stir in additional broth and Burgundy (1 part broth to 2 parts Burgundy). Add mushrooms and onions; heat through, stirring occasionally. Serve over noodles if desired.

12 SERVINGS

Liver and Onions in Milk Gravy

3 slices bacon, cut into ½-inch pieces
Vegetable oil
1 pound calf's liver, ½ to ¾ inch thick
¼ cup all-purpose flour
Salt and pepper
2 medium onions, thinly sliced
1 tablespoon all-purpose flour
1 cup milk

Cook bacon in 10-inch skillet until crisp. Remove bacon from skillet; reserve. Add oil, if necessary, to bacon fat in skillet to measure 3 tablespoons. Cut liver into serving pieces if necessary. Coat liver with ¼ cup flour. Cook liver in bacon fat over medium heat 5 to 6 minutes on each side or until almost done. Sprinkle with salt and pepper to taste. Remove liver from skillet; keep warm.

Cook and stir onions about 4 minutes or until tender. Sprinkle with 1 tablespoon flour; stir into onions. Pour milk over onions; reduce heat. Place liver on onion mixture. Cover and cook over low heat 6 to 8 minutes or until milk is slightly thickened. Sprinkle with reserved bacon.

4 SERVINGS

Red Flannel Hash

A hearty dish—originally made from leftovers—with a colorful past: Legend has it that Ethan Allen and his Green Mountain Boys enjoyed red flannel hash in Vermont, the Green Mountain State. The name is derived from the addition of chopped beets, which give it a ruby color reminiscent of soft red flannel. It is not uncommon to eat red flannel hash topped with a poached or fried egg.

2 cups chopped cooked corned beef brisket*
1½ cups chopped cooked potatoes (about
    1½ medium)
1½ cups diced cooked beets (about 12 ounces
    fresh beets)**
⅓ cup chopped onion
½ teaspoon salt
¼ teaspoon pepper
¼ cup shortening
Snipped fresh parsley

Mix all ingredients except shortening and parsley in large bowl. Heat shortening in 10-inch skillet over medium heat until melted. Spread beef mixture in skillet. Cook 10 to 15 minutes, turning occasionally with wide spatula, until brown. Sprinkle with parsley.

4 SERVINGS

*1 can (12 ounces) corned beef can be substituted for the brisket.

**1 can (16 ounces) diced beets, drained, can be substituted for the cooked beets.

Meat Loaf

Rolled oat flakes keep this family favorite juicy and tender. Warm from the oven, it's delicious accompanied by mashed or baked potatoes. Cold, it makes fabulous sandwiches. Either way, ketchup is the condiment of choice.

1 can (16 ounces) whole tomatoes
1¼ pounds ground beef
¼ pound ground pork
¾ cup regular oats
⅓ cup chopped onion
1 egg
1 teaspoon salt
¼ teaspoon pepper

Heat oven to 375°. Drain tomatoes, reserving ¼ cup liquid. Cut up tomatoes with fork. Mix tomato liquid and the remaining ingredients thoroughly. Pack in loaf pan, 8½ × 4½ × 2½ inches. Bake 1 hour.

6 TO 8 SERVINGS

Microwave Directions. Spread mixture evenly in microwavable loaf dish, 9 × 5 × 3 inches. Cover with waxed paper and microwave on medium-high (70%) 24 to 27 minutes, rotating dish ½ turn after 12 minutes, until center is no longer pink. Remove to serving platter; cover and let stand 5 minutes.

Roast Pork Loin with Yam-stuffed Apples

4-pound pork boneless top loin roast
½ teaspoon salt
½ teaspoon pepper
1 teaspoon dried sage, crushed
8 medium tart baking apples
1 yam or sweet potato (about 10 ounces), cooked
*   and mashed (about ¾ cup)*
¼ cup packed brown sugar
½ teaspoon salt
½ teaspoon ground cinnamon
2 tablespoons slivered almonds
2 tablespoons butter or margarine, melted
¼ cup maple syrup
Pork Gravy (below)

Heat oven to 325°. Sprinkle pork roast with salt and pepper; rub with sage. Place pork in shallow roasting pan. Insert meat thermometer so tip is in center of thickest part of pork and does not rest in fat. Roast uncovered 1 hour. Drain pan drippings; reserve.

Core each apple from stem end, making 1¼-inch diameter hole, leaving bottom of apple intact. Pare 1-inch strip around top of each. Mash pulp; mix with remaining ingredients except Pork Gravy. Fill apples with yam mixture. Arrange apples around pork. Bake about 1 hour or until meat thermometer registers 170°. Remove pork and apples to warm platter; keep warm. Prepare Pork Gravy; serve with pork and apples.

8 SERVINGS

PORK GRAVY

Strain reserved drippings and additional drippings from roasting pan. Remove fat; reserve 3 tablespoons. Add enough water to drippings to measure 2 cups liquid. Stir 3 tablespoons all-purpose flour into reserved fat in 1½-quart saucepan. Cook over low heat, stirring con-

stantly, until smooth and bubbly; remove from heat. Stir in liquid. Heat to boiling, stirring constantly. Boil and stir 1 minute.

Stuffed Pork Tenderloin

2 pork tenderloins (¾ to 1 pound each)
Salt and pepper
Bread Stuffing (below)
4 to 6 slices bacon

Heat oven to 350°. Make a cut lengthwise down center of each tenderloin; do not cut completely through. Spread tenderloins open. Season cut side of 1 tenderloin with salt and pepper; spread with stuffing. Place other tenderloin, cut side down, on stuffing; tie with string. Place on rack in shallow roasting pan. Place bacon slices in tenderloin. Insert meat thermometer so tip is in center of stuffing. Bake uncovered about 1 hour or until thermometer registers 165°.

6 TO 8 SERVINGS

BREAD STUFFING

½ cup chopped celery (stalk and leaves)
¼ cup finely chopped onion
⅓ cup butter or margarine
3 cups soft bread crumbs
1 teaspoon snipped fresh or ½ teaspoon
*   dried sage*
½ teaspoon snipped fresh or ¼ teaspoon
*   dried thyme*
½ teaspoon salt
⅛ teaspoon pepper

Cook and stir celery and onion in butter in 10-inch skillet until onion is tender. Stir in about 1 cup of the bread cubes. Turn into bowl; add remaining ingredients and toss.

Honey-baked Ham with Raisin Sauce

Cider, raisins and cloves lend autumnal flavor and sweet balance to the smoky ham. Hogs are natural scavengers and have traditionally been fed on leavings of all kinds, everything from surplus or unusable produce to table scraps. Down South, a diet of Virginia peanuts adds to the unique savor of a Smithfield ham. Heat slices of ham and serve with raisin sauce.

¼ cup honey
½ teaspoon dry mustard
¼ teaspoon ground cloves
5- to 7-pound fully cooked smoked ham
Whole cloves, if desired
Raisin Sauce (below)

Heat oven to 325°. Mix honey, mustard and cloves. Place ham, fat side up, on rack in shallow roasting pan. Insert meat thermometer so tip is in thickest part of ham and does not touch bone or rest in fat. Spoon or spread half of the honey mixture on ham. Bake 1½ to 2 hours or until heated through (140°). About 30 minutes before ham is done, remove from oven; pour drippings from pan. Cut fat surface of ham in uniform diamond pattern ¼ inch deep. Insert whole clove in each diamond. Spoon or spread remaining honey mixture on ham. Bake 30 minutes. Prepare Raisin Sauce; serve with ham.

10 TO 12 SERVINGS

RAISIN SAUCE

2 cups apple cider
2 tablespoons cornstarch
1 cup raisins
2 tablespoons butter or margarine

Stir apple cider gradually into cornstarch in 1½-quart saucepan. Add raisins and butter. Cook over medium heat, stirring constantly, until mixture thickens and boils. Boil and stir 1 minute. Serve warm.

Honey-glazed Ribs

4½ pounds fresh pork spareribs, cut into serving pieces
⅓ cup soy sauce
⅓ cup dry sherry or apple juice
2 tablespoons honey
1 clove garlic, finely chopped
½ cup honey

Place pork spareribs in plastic bag or shallow glass dish. Mix soy sauce, sherry, 2 tablespoons honey and the garlic; pour over pork. Fasten bag securely or cover dish with plastic wrap. Refrigerate at least 4 hours, turning pork occasionally. Remove pork from marinade; reserve marinade.

Heat oven to 325°. Place pork in jelly roll pan, 15½ × 10½ × 1 inch. Brush pork with marinade. Cover pan with aluminum foil. Bake 1 hour; remove foil. Bake about 1 hour, turning pork occasionally and basting with pan drippings, until pork is done. Brush with ½ cup honey.

6 SERVINGS

Honey-glazed Ribs

Scalloped Potatoes and Ham

This robust dish is a splendid way to use up left-over bits of cooked ham.

3 tablespoons butter or margarine
3 tablespoons all-purpose flour
½ teaspoon salt
¼ teaspoon pepper
2½ cups milk
6 cups thinly sliced potatoes (about 6 medium)
1 small onion, finely chopped (about ¼ cup)
1½ cups cubed fully cooked smoked ham
1 tablespoon butter or margarine

Heat oven to 350°. Grease 2-quart casserole. Heat 3 tablespoons butter in 1½-quart saucepan over low heat until melted. Stir in flour, salt and pepper. Cook over low heat, stirring constantly, until smooth and bubbly; remove from heat. Stir in milk. Heat to boiling, stirring constantly. Boil and stir 1 minute.

Layer ⅓ of the potatoes, ½ of the onion and ham and ⅓ of the white sauce in casserole; repeat. Top with remaining potatoes and white sauce. Dot with 1 tablespoon butter. Cover and bake 30 minutes. Uncover and bake 60 to 70 minutes or until potatoes are tender. Let stand 5 to 10 minutes before serving.

6 SERVINGS

Microwave Directions. Place 3 tablespoons butter, the flour, salt and pepper in 4-cup microwavable measure. Microwave on high 2 minutes, stirring after 1 minute, until very bubbly. Stir in milk gradually. Microwave 5 to 6 minutes, stirring with fork or wire whisk every 2 minutes, until thickened.

Layer as directed in 3-quart casserole. Omit 1 tablespoon butter. Cover tightly and microwave on medium-high (70%) 21 to 25 minutes, stirring every 6 minutes, until potatoes are tender. Let stand 5 minutes.

Ham Loaf with Red Currant Sauce

1 pound ground ham
¾ pound ground pork
1 cup soft bread crumbs
½ cup chopped onion
1 egg
½ cup milk
Red Currant Sauce (below)

Heat oven to 350°. Mix all ingredients except Red Currant Sauce. Shape mixture into loaf in ungreased rectangular pan, 13 × 9 × 2 inches. Bake uncovered 1 to 1¼ hours or until done. Prepare Red Currant Sauce. Remove ham loaf from pan; spoon Red Currant Sauce over ham loaf. Serve with any remaining sauce.

8 SERVINGS

RED CURRANT SAUCE

½ cup red currant jelly
1½ teaspoons grated orange peel
2 tablespoons orange juice
1 tablespoon prepared horseradish

Heat all ingredients, stirring occasionally, until jelly is melted and mixture is smooth.

Microwave Directions. Spread ham loaf mixture evenly in microwavable loaf dish, 9 × 5 × 3 inches. Cover with waxed paper and microwave on medium-high (70%) 27 to 30 minutes, rotating dish ½ turn after 12 minutes, until meat thermometer registers 170°. Remove to serving platter; cover and let stand 5 minutes.

Place sauce ingredients in 1-cup microwavable measure. Microwave uncovered on high 1 minute to 1 minute 30 seconds, stirring after 45 seconds, until jelly is melted. Stir until smooth.

Minted Leg of Lamb

Fresh mint is often used to flavor lamb, and recipes for mint sauces abound. Here, mint is added to a lemon marinade for a boned and rolled leg of lamb, suitable for roasting or grilling. The same marinade also adds a lift to lamb chops. Serve lots of mashed potatoes or cooked rice to capture every last bit of the gravy.

½ cup packed brown sugar
½ cup vegetable oil
1 teaspoon grated lemon peel
¼ cup lemon juice
3 tablespoons vinegar
¼ cup snipped fresh mint
1 tablespoon snipped fresh or 1 teaspoon
*   dried tarragon*
1 teaspoon salt
1 teaspoon dry mustard
4- to 5-pound leg of lamb, boned, rolled
*   and tied*
Lamb Gravy (right)

Mix all ingredients except leg of lamb and Lamb Gravy. Heat to boiling; reduce heat. Simmer 5 minutes; cool. Place lamb in plastic bag or shallow glass dish. Pour cooled marinade over lamb. Fasten bag securely or cover dish with plastic wrap. Refrigerate 24 hours, turning lamb occasionally.

Heat oven to 325°. Place lamb, fat side up, on rack in shallow roasting pan. Insert meat thermometer so tip is in center or thickest part of lamb and does not rest in fat. Roast uncovered 2 to 2½ hours or until desired degree of doneness. (Thermometer should register 170° to 180°.) Remove lamb to warm platter; keep warm. Prepare Lamb Gravy; serve with lamb.

8 SERVINGS

LAMB GRAVY

Strain drippings from roasting pan. Remove fat; reserve 2 tablespoons. Add enough water to drippings to measure 2 cups liquid. Stir 2 tablespoons all-purpose flour into reserved fat in 1½-quart saucepan. Cook over low heat, stirring constantly, until smooth and bubbly; remove from heat. Stir in liquid. Heat to boiling, stirring constantly. Boil and stir 1 minute.

Grilled Minted Leg of Lamb. Insert meat thermometer so tip is in center of thickest part of lamb and does not touch bone or rest in fat. Arrange hot coals around edge of firebox. Place water-filled foil drip pan under grilling area. Add fresh mint leaves to hot coals. Place lamb on grill about 4 inches from coals; cover grill. Cook 3 hours, adding fresh mint leaves at 30-minute intervals and hot coals if necessary, to maintain smoke and even heat, until desired degree of doneness. (Meat thermometer should register 170° to 180°.)

Stuffed Lamb Chops

½ cup finely chopped celery
½ cup chopped mushrooms
1 tablespoon finely chopped onion
2 tablespoons butter or margarine
1 tablespoon snipped fresh parsley
¼ teaspoon salt
½ cup dry bread crumbs
6 lamb loin chops, 1½ to 2 inches thick
    (5 to 6 ounces each)
2 eggs, slightly beaten
2 tablespoons milk
¾ cup fine dry bread crumbs
½ teaspoon salt
Dash of paprika
Mint jelly

Heat oven to 400°. Cook and stir celery, mushrooms and onion in butter until onion is tender. Stir in parsley, ¼ teaspoon salt and ½ cup bread crumbs.

Trim fat from lamb chops. Make a slit in each to form a pocket. Fill pocket with celery mixture. Dip each lamb chop into mixture of eggs and milk. Roll in mixture of ¾ cup bread crumbs, ½ teaspoon salt and the paprika. Place in ungreased rectangular pan, 13 × 9 × 2 inches. Bake uncovered 30 minutes; turn lamb chops over. Bake about 15 minutes or until lamb chops are tender. Serve with mint jelly.

6 SERVINGS

Stuffed Lamb Chops, Creamed Spinach (page 98) and Hoppin' John (page 74)

Chapter 4

SOUPS, BISQUES, CHOWDERS AND STEWS

*T*here is something about sitting before a steaming bowl of soup that says all is right with the world. Americans have traditionally enjoyed many different kinds of soups, but the classic distinctions seem to fade as the years go by.

A soup is the stock flavored by meat, seafood or vegetable, and it often contains solid pieces; the highlight of a soup is its broth. A stew is heartier than a soup, with larger or more numerous pieces of meat, seafood or vegetable; the more important part of a stew is what is in the broth. A chowder is a milk- or tomato-based soup or stew with seafood (fish, clams or mussels) or fresh corn; chowders are usually flavored with salt pork, onions and other vegetables (frequently potatoes). Finally, a bisque is the most elegant of all. Bisques are thick creamy soups, either based on vegetable purée or featuring small pieces of shellfish or game.

Historically, soups and the like came to the table "dressed." Croutons, little fried or toasted shapes of white bread, were frequently served atop soups. Snipped fresh chives are a delicious (and pretty) addition to many cold soups, and in the South, a dollop of whipped cream might grace an offering of cream of tomato soup. Don't forget to set out the soup spoons.

Lima Bean and Pork Hock Soup (page 57) and Sour Cream Biscuits (page 109)

Chicken and Slippery Noodle Soup

Homemade slippery noodles, also known as slick dumplings, are rolled thicker than traditional noodles, so they absorb lots of the flavorful broth in which they're cooked. That's why they require extra effort to get them from the bowl into your mouth!

Chicken and Broth (right)
2 cups all-purpose flour
½ cup water
2 tablespoons vegetable oil
½ teaspoon salt
2 medium carrots, sliced (about 1 cup)
2 medium stalks celery, sliced (about 1 cup)
1 small onion, chopped (about ¼ cup)

Prepare Chicken and Broth; reserve cut-up chicken. Mix flour, water, oil and salt in medium bowl. Stir in additional water, 1 tablespoon at a time, if necessary, until dough is stiff but easy to roll. Roll dough to ⅛-inch thickness on lightly floured surface. Cut into strips, 2 × 1 inches.

Add enough water to broth to measure 5 cups. Heat broth, chicken, carrots, celery and onion to boiling. Drop noodles, one at a time, into the boiling broth; reduce heat. Cover and simmer about 15 minutes or until carrots are tender. Let stand uncovered 10 minutes.

6 SERVINGS (ABOUT 1⅓ CUPS EACH)

CHICKEN AND BROTH

3- to 3½-pound broiler-fryer chicken, cut up
4½ cups cold water
1 teaspoon salt
½ teaspoon pepper
1 stalk celery with leaves, cut up
1 medium carrot, cut up
1 small onion, cut up
1 sprig fresh parsley

Remove any excess fat from chicken. Place chicken, giblets (except liver) and neck in Dutch oven. Add remaining ingredients; heat to boiling. Skim foam from broth; reduce heat. Cover and simmer about 45 minutes or until thickest pieces of chicken are done.

Remove chicken from broth; cool chicken about 10 minutes or just until cool enough to handle. Strain broth through cheesecloth-lined sieve. Remove chicken from bones and skin; cut up chicken. Discard bones, skin and vegetables. Skim fat from broth. Use immediately, or cover and refrigerate broth and chicken in separate containers up to 24 hours.

Lima Bean and Pork Hock Soup

*1 pound dried lima beans or great northern beans
    (about 2 cups)*
8 cups water
1 can (8 ounces) tomato sauce
2½ pounds smoked pork hocks or shanks
1 large onion, chopped (about 1 cup)
1 tablespoon beef bouillon granules
½ teaspoon pepper
3 cloves garlic, crushed
2 cups mashed cooked potatoes
2 cups shredded cabbage
*2 medium carrots, cut into ½-inch pieces
    (about 1 cup)*
2 tablespoons packed brown sugar
2 tablespoons prepared mustard

Heat beans and water to boiling in Dutch oven. Boil uncovered 2 minutes; remove from heat. Cover and let stand 1 hour.

Add tomato sauce, pork hocks, onion, bouillon granules, pepper and garlic to beans. Heat to boiling; reduce heat. Cover and simmer about 2 hours or until beans are tender (do not boil or beans will burst).

Remove pork from broth; cool about 10 minutes or just until cool enough to handle. Remove pork from bones; cut into ½-inch pieces. Skim fat from broth. Stir pork and remaining ingredients into broth. Heat to boiling; reduce heat. Cover and simmer about 45 minutes or until vegetables are tender.

10 SERVINGS (ABOUT 1½ CUPS EACH)

Vegetable Beef Soup

*1 pound beef boneless chuck, tip or round, cut
    into ½-inch cubes*
1 tablespoon vegetable oil
2 cups beef broth
1 teaspoon salt
*1½ teaspoons snipped fresh or ½ teaspoon
    dried marjoram*
*1½ teaspoons snipped fresh or ½ teaspoon
    dried thyme*
⅛ teaspoon pepper
1 bay leaf
3 cups water
1 cup whole kernel fresh, frozen or canned corn
3 medium carrots, sliced (about 1 cup)
1 large stalk celery, sliced (about ½ cup)
1 medium onion, chopped (about ½ cup)
1 can (16 ounces) whole tomatoes, undrained

Cook and stir beef in oil in Dutch oven over medium heat until brown. Stir in beef broth, salt, marjoram, thyme, pepper and bay leaf; reduce heat. Cover and simmer 1 to 1½ hours or until beef is tender.

Stir in water, corn, carrots, celery, onion and tomatoes. Heat to boiling; reduce heat. Cover and simmer about 35 minutes or until carrots are tender. Remove bay leaf.

5 SERVINGS (ABOUT 1½ CUPS EACH)

Vegetable Beef Soup and Fresh Herb Batter Bread (page 146)

Chicken and Corn Chowder

Although often prepared with fish or shellfish, a chowder is actually any rich soup, usually milk-based, that contains solid ingredients. This Pennsylvania Dutch recipe is thick with diced chicken, tender corn kernels and *rivels*, diminutive dumplings that are added just a few minutes before the chowder is served.

3- to 3½-pound broiler-fryer chicken, cut up
6 cups water
1 medium onion, sliced
3 medium stalks celery (with leaves), finely
    chopped (about 1½ cups)
1 medium carrot, chopped (about ½ cup)
2 teaspoons salt
1 can (17 ounces) cream-style corn
2 hard-cooked eggs, finely chopped
Egg Rivels (right)

Remove any excess fat from chicken. Place chicken, giblets (except liver) and neck in Dutch oven. Add water, onion, celery, carrot and salt; heat to boiling. Skim foam from broth; reduce heat. Cover and simmer about 1½ hours or until thickest pieces of chicken are done.

Remove chicken from broth; cool chicken about 10 minutes or just until cool enough to handle. Remove chicken from bones and skin; cut chicken into small pieces. Skim fat from broth; return chicken to broth. Stir in corn and eggs. Heat to boiling; reduce heat. Sprinkle with Egg Rivel mixture; stir into soup. Simmer uncovered 10 minutes.

8 SERVINGS (ABOUT 1⅓ CUPS EACH)

EGG RIVELS

1 cup all-purpose flour
¼ teaspoon salt
1 egg

Mix all ingredients until mixture looks like cornmeal.

Chicken and Dumplings

3- to 3½-pound stewing chicken, cut up
4 celery stalk tops
1 medium carrot, sliced
1 small onion, sliced
2 sprigs fresh parsley, snipped
1 teaspoon salt
⅛ teaspoon pepper
5 cups water
½ cup variety baking mix
2 cups variety baking mix
⅔ cup milk

Remove any excess fat from chicken. Place chicken, giblets (except liver), neck, celery, carrot, onion, parsley, salt, pepper and water in Dutch oven. Cover and heat to boiling; reduce heat. Cook over low heat about 2 hours or until chicken is done. Remove chicken and vegetables. Skim ½ cup fat from broth; reserve. Remove broth; reserve 4 cups. Heat reserved fat in Dutch oven; blend in ½ cup baking mix. Cook over low heat, stirring constantly, until mixture is smooth and bubbly; remove from heat. Stir in reserved broth. Heat to boiling, stirring constantly. Boil and stir 1 minute. Return chicken and vegetables to Dutch oven; heat through.

Mix 2 cups baking mix and the milk until soft dough forms. Drop by spoonfuls onto hot chicken mixture. Cook uncovered over low heat 10 minutes; cover and cook 10 minutes longer.

4 TO 6 SERVINGS

Shrimp Gumbo

Creole cooks in Louisiana devised the gumbo, a hearty soup traditionally thickened with either okra or filé powder. Filé powder, made from dried, pulverized sassafras leaves, must be added at the very end of the cooking time; otherwise it becomes stringy.

>2 cloves garlic, finely chopped
>2 medium onions, sliced
>½ medium green bell pepper, thinly sliced
>2 tablespoons butter or margarine
>12 ounces fresh okra, cut into ½-inch pieces*
>1 can (16 ounces) tomatoes, undrained
>1 can (6 ounces) tomato paste
>3 cups beef broth
>1 tablespoon Worcestershire sauce
>1 teaspoon salt
>1 teaspoon chili powder
>1 teaspoon snipped fresh or ½ teaspoon
>   dried basil
>¼ teaspoon pepper
>1 bay leaf
>1½ pounds cleaned raw shrimp**
>1 tablespoon filé powder
>3 cups hot cooked rice

Cook and stir garlic, onions and bell pepper in butter in Dutch oven over medium heat until tender. Stir in okra, tomatoes, tomato paste, broth, Worcestershire sauce, salt, chili powder, basil, pepper and bay leaf. Break up tomatoes with fork. Heat to boiling; reduce heat. Simmer uncovered 45 minutes. Stir in shrimp. Cover and simmer 5 minutes or until shrimp are pink and tender. Remove bay leaf; stir in filé powder. Serve with hot cooked rice.

8 SERVINGS (ABOUT 1 CUP EACH)

*1 package (10 ounces) frozen okra may be substituted for the fresh okra.
**About 1¾ pounds fresh or frozen raw shrimp in shells.

Beef Stew

For even cooking, cut the meat into cubes of the same size. The variance in flour at the end of the recipe depends on the desired thickness of the gravy; 1 tablespoon will produce a thin sauce, 2 tablespoons a thicker one. Like most stews, this one reheats well.

>¼ cup all-purpose flour
>1½ teaspoons salt
>⅛ teaspoon pepper
>1½ pounds beef stew meat, cut into
>   1½-inch pieces
>2 tablespoons vegetable oil
>⅓ cup chopped onion
>2 cups water
>1 cup beef broth
>3 medium potatoes, pared and cut into fourths
>2 medium onions, cut into fourths
>2 carrots, cut into 1-inch slices
>½ cup fresh, frozen or canned green peas
>½ cup cold water
>1 to 2 tablespoons all-purpose flour
>Snipped fresh parsley

Mix ¼ cup flour, the salt and pepper. Coat beef with flour mixture. Heat oil in Dutch oven until hot; cook beef until brown. Stir in chopped onion. Cook 5 minutes, stirring frequently; drain.

Add water and broth. Heat to boiling; reduce heat. Cover and simmer 2 hours. Stir in potatoes, onions, carrots and peas. Cover and simmer about 30 minutes or until vegetables are tender. Shake ½ cup cold water and 1 to 2 tablespoons flour in tightly covered container; stir into stew. Heat to boiling, stirring constantly. Boil and stir 1 minute. Sprinkle with parsley.

4 TO 6 SERVINGS

Shrimp Gumbo and Hush Puppies (page 114)

Brunswick Stew

Once prepared with squirrel and other small woodland mammals, this rustic stew evolved into a dish usually made with chicken or turkey and a variety of vegetables. Still popular in its native Brunswick County, Virginia, it is often cooked in great steaming kettles and served at outdoor gatherings.

3- to 3½-pound broiler-fryer chicken, cut up
2 cups water
1 teaspoon salt
¼ teaspoon pepper
Dash of ground red pepper
2 cans (16 ounces each) whole tomatoes,
*   undrained*
1 can (17 ounces) whole kernel corn, undrained
1 can (14 ounces) lima beans, undrained
1 medium potato, cut into cubes (about 1 cup)
1 medium onion, chopped (about ½ cup)
¼ pound lean salt pork, cut into 1-inch pieces
½ cup water
2 tablespoons all-purpose flour

Remove any excess fat from chicken. Heat chicken, giblets (except liver), neck, 2 cups water and salt to boiling in Dutch oven; reduce heat. Cover and simmer about 1 hour or until thickest pieces of chicken are done.

Remove chicken from broth; cool chicken about 10 minutes or just until cool enough to handle. Skim fat from broth. Remove skin and bones from chicken if desired; return chicken to broth. Stir in pepper, red pepper, tomatoes, corn, beans, potato, onion and salt pork. Heat to boiling; reduce heat. Simmer uncovered 1 hour. Shake ½ cup water and the flour in tightly covered container. Stir into stew. Heat to boiling, stirring constantly. Boil and stir 1 minute.

8 SERVINGS

Bouillabaisse

Serve lots of crusty French bread to mop up the flavorful broth, or ladle the soup over a thick slice of toasted, crusty bread.

1 cup chopped onion
¼ cup chopped carrot
1 clove garlic, finely chopped
½ cup vegetable oil
3 pounds frozen fish fillets, thawed and cut into
*   3-inch pieces*
1 can (16 ounces) whole tomatoes, undrained
2 bay leaves
2 quarts water
6 fresh or frozen lobster tails, cut lengthwise
*   into halves*
1 pound fresh or frozen shelled raw shrimp
1 can (10 ounces) whole clams, undrained
1 can (10½ ounces) beef broth
½ cup chopped pimiento
¼ cup snipped fresh parsley
1 tablespoon salt
1 tablespoon lemon juice
½ teaspoon saffron
Dash of pepper

Cook and stir onion, carrot and garlic in vegetable oil in Dutch oven about 10 minutes or until onion is tender. Add fish, tomatoes, bay leaves and water. Heat to boiling; reduce heat. Cover and simmer 30 minutes. Stir in remaining ingredients; cover and simmer 30 minutes. Remove bay leaves. Serve in large bowls with French bread if desired.

ABOUT 10 SERVINGS

Chapter 5

POTATOES, GRAINS, MACARONI AND EGGS

*I*t is doubtful that any more reliable vegetable than the potato exists. *Potatoes are long-keeping, satisfying and nutritious. They lend themselves to hundreds of preparations, using every cooking technique from frying to steaming. Perhaps we riced them more often in days gone by than we do today, but our admiration for hot mashed potatoes, rich with milk or cream and with little rivers of gravy, is as fervent as ever.*

Grains and macaroni (what is called, in our current sophistication, "pasta") too are cozy foods. Whether it's Carolina rice or Eastern navy beans, Southern grits or Hoppin' John, there is always a little room on the plate for a good-sized spoonful or two.

Lemon-Parsley New Potatoes (page 70), Poached Salmon with Hollandaise Sauce (page 26) and Sweet Summer Peas (page 96)

Lemon-Parsley New Potatoes

2¼ pounds new potatoes (15 to 18 small)
3 tablespoons butter or margarine
1 tablespoon snipped fresh parsley
1 teaspoon grated lemon peel
¼ teaspoon salt
⅛ teaspoon pepper

Pare a strip from the center of each potato. Heat 1 inch salted water (¼ teaspoon salt, if desired, to 1 cup water) to boiling in 3-quart saucepan; add potatoes. Cover and heat to boiling; reduce heat. Cook 20 to 25 minutes or until tender; drain. Return potatoes to saucepan.

Heat butter until melted; stir in remaining ingredients. Pour over potatoes; stir gently to coat.

4 SERVINGS

Microwave Directions. Stir ½ cup water and ¼ teaspoon salt in 2-quart microwavable casserole until salt is dissolved. Place potatoes in casserole, arranging larger potatoes at outside edge of casserole, small potatoes in center. Cover tightly and microwave on high 12 to 14 minutes, stirring after 5 minutes, until potatoes are tender. Let stand 3 minutes; drain. Continue as directed.

Potato Chips

Potato chips got their start as "Saratoga chips," named for their birthplace, the resort Saratoga Springs in New York State. In order to satisfy a difficult customer, George Crum, the Native American chef of Moon's Lake House, prepared French fried potatoes sliced so thinly that they became mere crisps.

4 medium potatoes
Vegetable oil
Salt

Slice potatoes as thinly as possible. Soak in cold water 1 hour; drain and pat dry.

Heat oil (1 inch) in Dutch oven to 375°. Fry 12 to 15 potato slices at a time 2 to 4 minutes, turning if necessary, until golden brown; drain on paper towels. Sprinkle with salt.

7 TO 8 CUPS

Applesauce–Sweet Potato Bake

1 pound fresh sweet potatoes or yams
*   (about 3 medium)**
1 cup applesauce
⅓ cup packed brown sugar
¼ cup chopped nuts
½ teaspoon ground cinnamon
2 tablespoons butter or margarine

Place sweet potatoes in saucepan; add enough salted water (¼ teaspoon salt, if desired, to 1 cup water) to cover. Heat to boiling; reduce heat. Cover and cook 30 to 35 minutes or until tender; drain. Remove skins; cut each sweet potato lengthwise into halves.

Heat oven to 375°. Place sweet potatoes, cut sides up, in ungreased square baking dish, 8 × 8 × 2 inches. Spread applesauce over sweet potatoes. Stir together brown sugar, nuts and cinnamon; sprinkle over applesauce. Dot with butter. Cover with aluminum foil. Bake 30 minutes or until hot.

4 TO 6 SERVINGS

*1 can (18 ounces) vacuum-pack sweet potatoes, halved lengthwise, can be substituted for the fresh sweet potatoes.

Microwave Directions. Pierce sweet potatoes several times with fork. Arrange potatoes about 2 inches apart in triangle on microwavable paper towel in microwave oven. Microwave uncovered on high 5 to 7 minutes or until tender when pierced with fork. Let stand 5 minutes. Remove skins; cut each sweet potato lengthwise into halves.

Arrange sweet potatoes, cut sides up, in square microwavable dish, 8 × 8 × 2 inches; spread applesauce over sweet potatoes. Stir together brown sugar, nuts and cinnamon; sprinkle over applesauce. Dot with butter. Cover with waxed paper. Microwave on medium-high (70%) 7 to 9 minutes, spooning liquid from dish over potatoes after 4 minutes, until liquid is hot and bubbly.

Oven-browned Potatoes

These crusty potatoes are meant to be cooked with a roast. They could just as easily be baked by themselves on a rack over a broiler pan, if desired.

6 medium potatoes, pared
½ cup butter or margarine, if desired

About 1½ hours before roast is done, cut each potato diagonally into ½-inch slices, being careful not to cut completely through bottom; repeat in opposite direction. Heat 1 inch salted water (¼ teaspoon salt, if desired, to 1 cup water) to boiling; add potatoes. Cover and heat to boiling; reduce heat. Cook 10 minutes; drain.

Place potatoes in drippings in pan, turning each potato to coat completely. Or brush potatoes with butter or margarine, melted; place on rack with roast. Continue cooking about 1¼ hours, turning potatoes once, until tender and golden brown. Sprinkle with salt and pepper.

6 SERVINGS

Hash Brown Potatoes

These golden brown shreds, delicately seasoned with onion, are equally delicious with eggs for breakfast or steak for supper. For many years they were standard fare at American roadside diners. Serve in wedges, or present the whole round at the table, then cut into serving pieces.

> 1½ pounds potatoes (about 4 medium), pared
> 2 tablespoons finely chopped onion
> ½ teaspoon salt
> ⅛ teaspoon pepper
> 2 tablespoons butter or margarine
> 2 tablespoons vegetable oil or bacon fat

Heat 1 inch salted water (¼ teaspoon salt, if desired, to 1 cup water) to boiling; add potatoes. Cover and heat to boiling; reduce heat. Cook 30 to 35 minutes or until tender; drain and cool slightly. Shred enough to measure 4 cups.

Toss potatoes, onion, salt and pepper. Heat butter and oil in 10-inch skillet until butter is melted. Pack potato mixture firmly in skillet, leaving a ½-inch space around edge. Cook over low heat 10 to 15 minutes or until bottom is brown. Cut potato mixture into fourths; turn. Add 1 tablespoon vegetable oil if necessary. Cook 12 to 15 minutes or until bottom is brown.

4 SERVINGS

Note. Potato mixture can be kept in one piece if desired. To turn, invert on plate and slide back into skillet.

Mashed Potatoes

Served just as they are, mashed potatoes are comfort fare at its best. As Duchess Potatoes, they are transformed into an elegant addition to a company meat platter.

> 2 pounds potatoes (about 6 medium), pared
> ⅓ to ½ cup milk
> ¼ cup butter or margarine, softened
> ½ teaspoon salt
> Dash of pepper

Heat 1 inch salted water (¼ teaspoon salt, if desired, to 1 cup water) to boiling; add potatoes. Cover and heat to boiling; reduce heat. Cook whole potatoes 30 to 35 minutes, potato pieces 20 to 25 minutes or until tender; drain. Shake pan gently over low heat to dry potatoes.

Mash potatoes until no lumps remain. Beat in milk in small amounts. (Amount of milk needed to make potatoes smooth and fluffy depends on kind of potatoes.) Add butter, salt and pepper; beat vigorously until potatoes are light and fluffy. Dot with butter or sprinkle with paprika, snipped parsley, watercress or chives if desired.

5 SERVINGS

Duchess Potatoes. Heat oven to 425°. Beat 2 eggs; add to Mashed Potatoes and beat until blended. Drop mixture by spoonfuls in mounds onto ungreased cookie sheet, or from rosettes, using decorators' tube with tip. Brush mounds or rosettes with melted butter or margarine. Bake uncovered about 15 minutes or until potatoes are light brown.

ABOUT 10 MOUNDS OR ROSETTES

Baked Beans

The weekly ritual of preparing baked beans for the Puritan Sabbath gave Boston the nickname "Beantown." Housewives combined the ingredients, had them baked slowly in a communal oven, then served them at Saturday supper or Sunday breakfast. For a real New England touch, pierce a peeled onion with several whole cloves and bury it in the middle of the beans before baking.

1 pound dried navy beans (about 2 cups)
6 cups water
¾ pound lean salt pork or smoked pork, sliced
½ cup chopped onion
2 cloves garlic, finely chopped
½ teaspoon red pepper sauce
1 bay leaf, crumbled
¼ cup ketchup
¼ cup molasses
1½ teaspoons dry mustard
½ teaspoon salt
½ teaspoon ground ginger
1½ teaspoons Worcestershire sauce
⅓ cup packed dark brown sugar

Heat beans and water to boiling. Boil uncovered 2 minutes; remove from heat. Cover; let stand 1 hour.

Stir in pork, onion, garlic, pepper sauce and bay leaf. Heat to boiling; reduce heat. Cover and simmer 1½ to 2 hours or until beans are tender (do not boil or beans will burst).

Heat oven to 400°. Drain beans, reserving liquid. Add enough water, if necessary, to measure 2 cups. Stir ketchup, molasses, mustard, salt, ginger and Worcestershire sauce into bean liquid. Place beans in ungreased shallow 2-quart casserole; pour reserved bean liquid over beans. Arrange pork slices on top; sprinkle with brown sugar. Bake uncovered 1 hour.

6 SERVINGS

Hoppin' John

In the South, a year of good luck is said to come to all who eat dried peas on New Year's Day. This dish of black-eyed peas, bacon or salt pork and rice is the traditional way to ensure a bright future. Serve with hot buttered corn bread.

½ pound dried black-eyed peas (about 1 cup)
3½ cups water
¼ pound slab bacon, lean salt pork or smoked pork
1 onion, sliced
¼ to ½ teaspoon very finely chopped fresh hot pepper or ⅛ to ¼ teaspoon crushed red pepper
½ cup uncooked long-grain rice
1 teaspoon salt
Pepper

Heat peas and water to boiling in 2-quart saucepan. Boil uncovered 2 minutes; remove from heat. Cover and let stand 1 hour.

Cut bacon into 8 pieces. Stir bacon, onion and red pepper into peas. Heat to boiling; reduce heat. Cover and simmer 1 to 1½ hours or until peas are tender (do not boil or peas will burst). Stir in rice, salt and pepper. Cover and simmer about 25 minutes, stirring occasionally, until rice is tender. Stir in additional water, if necessary, to cook rice.

6 TO 8 SERVINGS

Spanish Rice

1 cup uncooked regular rice
1 medium onion, chopped (about ½ cup)
2 tablespoons vegetable oil
2½ cups water
1 can (8 ounces) tomato sauce
1 small green bell pepper, chopped
    (about ½ cup)
1½ teaspoons salt
¾ teaspoon chili powder
⅛ teaspoon garlic powder

Cook and stir rice and onion in oil in 10-inch skillet until rice is golden brown and onion is tender. Stir in remaining ingredients. Heat to boiling; reduce heat. Cover and simmer about 30 minutes, stirring occasionally, until rice is tender.

6 SERVINGS

Savory Pilaf

1 small onion, chopped (about ¼ cup)
2 tablespoons butter or margarine
1 cup uncooked regular rice
2 cups chicken broth
1 package (6 ounces) diced dried fruits
    and raisins
¼ teaspoon salt
¼ teaspoon ground mace
¼ cup slivered almonds, toasted

Cook and stir onion in butter in 3-quart saucepan over medium-low heat until onion is tender. Stir in rice. Cook and stir 5 minutes. Stir in remaining ingredients except almonds. Heat to boiling, stirring once or twice; reduce heat. Cover and simmer 16 minutes (do not lift cover or stir); remove from heat. Stir in almonds. Cover and let steam 5 to 10 minutes.

8 SERVINGS

Microwave Directions. Place onion, butter and rice in 3-quart microwavable casserole. Microwave uncovered on high 2 to 3 minutes, stirring after 1 minute, until onion is tender. Increase chicken broth to 2¼ cups. Stir in remaining ingredients except almonds. Cover tightly and microwave 18 to 21 minutes, stirring after 10 minutes, until rice is tender. Stir in almonds.

Rice Croquettes with Parsley Sauce

Parsley Sauce (below)
Vegetable oil
2 cups cold cooked white or brown rice
¼ cup grated Parmesan cheese
1 tablespoon snipped fresh parsley
⅛ teaspoon pepper
2 green onions (with tops), chopped
2 eggs
2 teaspoons milk
½ cup dry bread crumbs

Prepare Parsley Sauce; keep warm. Heat oil (1 inch) in Dutch oven to 350°. Mix rice, cheese, parsley, pepper, green onions and 1 egg in large bowl. Mix remaining egg and the milk in small bowl. Shape rice mixture into 12 ovals, using about 1 rounded tablespoon per oval. Dip into egg mixture; coat with bread crumbs. Fry 2 to 3 minutes on each side or until deep golden brown; drain on paper towels. Serve with Parsley Sauce.

6 SERVINGS

PARSLEY SAUCE

1 tablespoon butter or margarine
1 tablespoon all-purpose flour
¼ teaspoon salt
⅛ teaspoon pepper
1 cup milk
2 tablespoons snipped fresh parsley

Heat butter in 1½-quart saucepan over low heat until melted. Stir in flour, salt and pepper. Cook over low heat, stirring constantly, until smooth and bubbly; remove from heat. Stir in milk and parsley. Heat to boiling, stirring constantly. Boil and stir 1 minute.

Grits Casserole

5 cups water
1½ cups quick-cooking grits
2 cups shredded Cheddar cheese (8 ounces)
¼ cup butter or margarine
1 teaspoon salt
¼ teaspoon red pepper sauce
1 clove garlic, crushed
3 eggs, slightly beaten

Heat oven to 350°. Heat water to boiling in 3-quart saucepan. Stir in grits gradually. Heat to boiling; reduce heat. Cook uncovered about 5 minutes, stirring occasionally, until thick; remove from heat.

Stir in cheese, butter, salt, pepper sauce and garlic. Stir about ¼ of the hot mixture into eggs; stir into remaining hot mixture in saucepan. Spread in ungreased rectangular baking dish, 11 × 7 × 1½ inches. Bake uncovered about 40 minutes or until firm and knife inserted in center comes out clean.

10 SERVINGS

Microwave Directions. Microwave water uncovered on high in 3-quart casserole 3 to 5 minutes or until hot. Stir in grits and salt. Microwave 10 to 12 minutes, stirring after 5 minutes, until thick.

Stir in cheese, butter, pepper sauce and garlic until cheese is melted. Stir about ¼ of the hot mixture into eggs; stir into hot mixture in casserole. Microwave uncovered 16 to 18 minutes or until set and knife inserted in center comes out clean.

Polenta with Tomato Sauce

A dish known to the northern Italians as polenta is more commonly called cornmeal mush in the American South. Depending on the amount of liquid used, polenta can can be as soft as mashed potatoes or as firm as bread pudding. Soft versions of it are often topped with syrup or milk and honey. When prepared in the following manner, the polenta is firm enough to slice and serve with a savory sauce. To prevent lumps, the cornmeal is first combined with cold water before boiling water is added.

1 cup yellow cornmeal
1 cup cold water
2 cups boiling water
½ teaspoon salt
1 cup shredded Cheddar cheese (4 ounces)
Tomato Sauce (right)

Grease loaf pan, 9 × 5 × 3 inches. Mix cornmeal and 1 cup cold water in 2-quart saucepan. Stir in 2 cups boiling water and salt. Cook, stirring constantly, until mixture thickens and boils; reduce heat. Cover and simmer 10 minutes, stirring occasionally. Stir in cheese until melted. Pour into pan. Let stand at room temperature 25 to 30 minutes or until set.

Prepare Tomato Sauce. Loosen edges of polenta and unmold. Cut into 12 slices, about ½ inch thick. Serve with Tomato Sauce. Garnish with 2 tablespoons bacon reserved from Tomato Sauce.

6 SERVINGS

TOMATO SAUCE

4 slices bacon, cut up
¼ cup chopped onion
¼ cup chopped green bell pepper
2 tablespoons all-purpose flour
1 tablespoon sugar
⅛ teaspoon pepper
1 can (15 ounces) tomato sauce

Cook bacon in 1½-quart saucepan, stirring occasionally, until brown. Remove bacon; reserve. Cook onion and bell pepper in bacon fat, stirring occasionally, until tender. Stir in flour, sugar and pepper. Cook over low heat, stirring constantly, until bubbly. Boil and stir 1 minute. Stir in tomato sauce and all except 2 tablespoons of the reserved bacon.

Macaroni and Cheese

A dish loved by old and young alike, macaroni and cheese can be enriched with bits of cooked ham, bacon or vegetables. For a crunchy topping, sprinkle it with a layer of buttered bread crumbs before placing it in the oven. Thomas Jefferson is said to have experimented with variations on the theme of macaroni and cheese.

2 cups uncooked elbow macaroni (8 ounces)
¼ cup butter or margarine
¼ cup all-purpose flour
½ teaspoon salt
¼ teaspoon pepper
¼ teaspoon dry mustard
¼ teaspoon Worcestershire sauce
2 cups milk
2 cups shredded or cubed sharp Cheddar cheese
    (8 ounces)

Cook macaroni as directed on package; drain and reserve. Heat oven to 350°. Heat butter in 3-quart saucepan over low heat until melted. Stir in flour, salt, pepper, mustard and Worcestershire sauce. Cook over low heat, stirring constantly, until mixture is smooth and bubbly; remove from heat. Stir in milk. Heat to boiling, stirring constantly. Boil and stir 1 minute. Add cheese; cook, stirring occasionally, until melted. Stir in reserved macaroni gently. Pour into ungreased 2-quart casserole. Bake uncovered 20 to 25 minutes or until bubbly.

6 SERVINGS

Macaroni Ring with Creamed Peas

2 cups uncooked elbow macaroni (8 ounces)
2 cups hot milk
¼ cup butter or margarine
2 cups shredded Cheddar cheese (8 ounces)
2 cups soft bread crumbs
2 eggs, slightly beaten
2 tablespoons snipped fresh parsley
2 tablespoons finely chopped onion
2 tablespoons chopped pimiento
½ teaspoon salt
¼ teaspoon pepper
Creamed Peas (right)

Cook macaroni as directed on package; drain. Heat oven to 350°. Grease 10-inch ring mold. Mix macaroni and remaining ingredients except Creamed Peas. Pour into mold; place in pan of very hot water (1 inch deep). Bake 35 to 40 minutes or until set. Remove mold from water; let stand 5 minutes. Loosen sides with metal spatula. Unmold ring on large platter; fill center with Creamed Peas.

8 SERVINGS

CREAMED PEAS

2 pounds fresh green peas*
2 tablespoons finely chopped onion
2 tablespoons butter or margarine
2 tablespoons all-purpose flour
¼ teaspoon salt
1½ cups milk

Heat 1 inch salted water (¼ teaspoon salt, if desired, to 1 cup water) to boiling; add peas. Heat to boiling; reduce heat. Cook uncovered 5 minutes. Cover and cook 3 to 7 minutes or until tender; drain.

Cook and stir onion in butter in 2-quart saucepan until tender. Stir in flour and salt. Cook over low heat, stirring constantly, until mixture is bubbly; remove from heat. Stir in milk. Heat to boiling, stirring constantly. Boil and stir 1 minute. Stir in peas gently; heat through.

*1 package (10 ounces) frozen green peas, cooked and drained, or 1 can (16 ounces) green peas, drained, can be substituted for the fresh green peas.

Macaroni Ring with Creamed Peas

Scotch Eggs

A popular pub and picnic treat all over the British Isles, these sausage-encased eggs were mentioned in the 1880 edition of *Miss Parloa's New Cook Book,* published by Washburn-Crosby Co. Miss Parloa liked her food good and spicy: She added "cayenne enough to cover a silver five-cent piece," or a generous ⅛ of a teaspoon.

>*4 eggs*
>*2 teaspoons all-purpose flour*
>*Dash of salt and pepper*
>*½ pound bulk pork sausage*
>*1 egg, beaten*
>*Dry bread crumbs*
>*Vegetable oil*

Place 4 eggs in saucepan; add enough cold water to come at least 1 inch above eggs. Heat rapidly to boiling; remove from heat. Cover and let stand 22 to 24 minutes. Cool eggs immediately in cold water to prevent further cooking; peel.

Mix flour, salt and pepper. Roll peeled eggs in flour mixture. Pat pork around each egg with wet hands. Dip into beaten egg, then into bread crumbs. Roll gently on waxed paper to remove excess crumbs.

Heat oil (1 to 1½ inches) in 3-quart saucepan to 375°. Fry eggs in hot oil 5 minutes; drain on paper towels.

4 SERVINGS

Deviled Eggs

Although there's no documented proof that deviled eggs were invented as a way to use up hard-cooked Easter eggs, it certainly is a fine solution. Deviled or stuffed eggs have long played a classic role at American picnics.

>*6 eggs*
>*3 tablespoons mayonnaise, salad dressing*
>   *or half-and-half*
>*1 teaspoon prepared horseradish*
>*½ teaspoon dry mustard*
>*¼ teaspoon pepper*
>*⅛ teaspoon salt*
>*Paprika*

Place eggs in saucepan; add enough cold water to come at least 1 inch above eggs. Heat rapidly to boiling; remove from heat. Cover and let stand 22 to 24 minutes. Cool eggs immediately in cold water to prevent further cooking; peel.

Cut peeled eggs lengthwise into halves. Slip out yolks; mash with fork. Mix in mayonnaise, horseradish, mustard, pepper and salt. Fill whites with egg yolk mixture, heaping it lightly. Sprinkle with paprika.

6 SERVINGS

Scotch Eggs and Deviled Eggs

VEGETABLES, FRUITS AND SALADS

*T*he Washburn-Crosby Co. Gold Medal Flour Cook Book *(published in 1910)* advises, *"Green vegetables should be cooked as soon after picking as possible, otherwise they should be spread on [the] floor of a dry and well ventilated cellar or placed in the ice box." Few city dwellers have the luxury of a "dry and well ventilated cellar," but most of us have refrigerators and nearly all of us enjoy the availability (unmatched anywhere else in the world) of beautiful produce, much of it to be had year 'round. But in the olden days, the staying power of sturdy root vegetables was a blessing.*

It is certainly more common today to find vegetables, and even fruits, the focus of a light meal. In most households, however, it used to be that the "side dishes" played a role of substance. It was common for two, three or even more "sides" to appear at a meal. The variety, reflecting so many seasonal foods that today we take for granted, is astounding. From hearty Maple-baked Squash to crisp Coleslaw, from cool Sour Cream Cucumbers to sweet Baked Honey Onions, the collection that follows has coaxed even the most adamant, vegetable-resisting children for more than 100 years.

Sweet-and-Sour Green Beans (page 86) and Corn Bread–stuffed Trout (page 25)

Sweet-and-Sour Green Beans

Bacon adds a nice smoky undertone to this German-style treatment for beans. Today's sweet-and-sour dishes are a bit more sour and a bit less sweet, to reflect current tastes. If you prefer things on the sweeter side, by all means add a little more sugar.

> 10 ounces fresh green beans, cut into
>   1-inch pieces*
> 2 slices bacon, cut up
> 1 medium onion, finely chopped (about ½ cup)
> 1 tablespoon all-purpose flour
> ½ cup water
> ¼ cup white or cider vinegar
> 2 tablespoons sugar
> ¼ teaspoon salt
> ¼ teaspoon pepper

Place beans in 1 inch salted water (¼ teaspoon salt, if desired, to 1 cup water). Heat to boiling; reduce heat. Boil uncovered 5 minutes. Cover and boil 4 to 6 minutes or until desired tenderness; drain.

Cook bacon in 10-inch skillet, stirring occasionally, until crisp; remove bacon. Drain fat from skillet, reserving 1 tablespoon. Cook and stir onion in bacon fat about 3 minutes or until onion is tender. Stir in flour; add remaining ingredients except beans. Heat to boiling, stirring constantly. Boil and stir 1 minute. Stir in beans. Cook until beans are heated through. Sprinkle with bacon.

4 SERVINGS

2 cups frozen cut green beans, cooked and drained, or 1 can (16 ounces) cut green beans, drained, can be substituted for the fresh beans.

Creamy Green Bean Casserole

A superb accompaniment to roast beef, this crunch-topped casserole can be assembled ahead of time and refrigerated for a couple of hours.

> 1 pound fresh green beans, cut into 1-inch pieces*
> 1 cup sour cream
> 2 tablespoons all-purpose flour
> ¾ teaspoon salt
> ¼ teaspoon pepper
> ¼ cup milk
> 2 tablespoons grated onion
> ⅓ cup dry bread crumbs
> 2 tablespoons butter or margarine, melted

Heat oven to 350°. Place beans in 1 inch salted water (¼ teaspoon salt, if desired, to 1 cup water). Heat to boiling; reduce heat. Boil uncovered 5 minutes. Cover and boil 4 to 6 minutes or until desired tenderness; drain.

Mix sour cream, flour, salt and pepper in ungreased 1½-quart casserole. Stir in milk, onion and beans. Mix bread crumbs and butter. Sprinkle over bean mixture. Bake uncovered about 30 minutes or until bread crumbs are light brown.

6 SERVINGS

4 cups frozen cut green beans, cooked and drained, or 2 cans (16 ounces each) cut green beans, drained, can be substituted for the fresh beans.

Beets with Orange Sauce

¼ cup packed brown sugar
1 tablespoon cornstarch
⅛ teaspoon salt
⅛ teaspoon pepper
¾ cup orange juice
1 tablespoon butter or margarine
1 can (16 ounces) diced beets, drained
1 teaspoon grated orange peel

Mix brown sugar, cornstarch, salt and pepper in saucepan. Stir in orange juice gradually; add butter. Cook, stirring constantly, until mixture thickens and boils. Boil and stir 1 minute. Stir in beets; heat through. Sprinkle with orange peel.

4 SERVINGS

Microwave Directions. Decrease orange juice to ½ cup. Mix brown sugar, cornstarch, salt, pepper, butter and orange juice in 1-quart microwavable casserole. Stir in beets. Cover tightly and microwave on high 4 to 5 minutes, stirring after 2 minutes, until sauce thickens. Sprinkle with orange peel.

Broccoli with Cheese

1½ pounds fresh broccoli
6 ounces process American cheese, shredded
¼ cup sliced almonds, toasted

Cut thick broccoli stems, lengthwise into fourths. Heat 1 inch salted water (¼ teaspoon salt, if desired, to 1 cup water) to boiling; add broccoli. Cover and heat to boiling; reduce heat. Cook 5 to 8 minutes or until stems are tender; drain. Arrange half of the broccoli in serving dish. Sprinkle with half of the cheese and almonds; repeat.

6 SERVINGS

Microwave Directions. Mix ¼ cup water and ¼ teaspoon salt until salt is dissolved; pour into rectangular microwavable baking dish, 12 × 7½ × 2 inches. Arrange broccoli with tips in center of dish. Cover with vented plastic wrap and microwave on high 7 to 9 minutes, rotating dish ½ turn after 4 minutes, until stems are tender; drain. Continue as directed.

Quick Crispy Cabbage

1 medium head green cabbage (about
    1½ pounds), shredded (about 7½ cups)
½ cup milk
1 tablespoon butter or margarine
½ teaspoon salt
Dash of pepper

Heat cabbage and milk to simmering in 10-inch skillet over medium heat, stirring frequently. Cover and cook about 5 minutes, stirring occasionally, until cabbage is crisp-tender. Stir in butter, salt and pepper.

4 SERVINGS

Microwave Directions. Decrease milk to ⅓ cup. Place cabbage, milk, butter, salt and pepper in 2-quart microwavable casserole. Cover tightly and microwave on high 6 to 7 minutes, stirring after 4 minutes, until cabbage is crisp-tender.

Ginger-glazed Carrots

Much of the crystallized ginger available today comes from Australia. Its spicy sweetness adds zing to vegetable and fruit dishes. Store the ginger in a tightly covered container to keep it soft and moist.

> *3 cups sliced carrots*
> *¼ cup sugar*
> *2 tablespoons butter or margarine*
> *1 teaspoon finely chopped crystallized ginger*

Heat 1 inch salted water (¼ teaspoon salt, if desired, to 1 cup water) to boiling in 3-quart saucepan; add carrots. Heat to boiling; reduce heat. Cover and cook about 5 minutes or until crisp-tender; drain.

Cook and stir sugar, butter and ginger in same saucepan until bubbly; add carrots. Cook 1 to 2 minutes over low heat, stirring occasionally, until carrots are glazed and heated through.

6 SERVINGS

Microwave Directions. Place carrots and 2 tablespoons water in 1½-quart microwavable casserole. Cover tightly and microwave on high 4 to 6 minutes, stirring after 2 minutes, until carrots are crisp-tender; drain. Stir in sugar, butter and ginger. Cover and microwave 2 to 3 minutes, stirring after 1 minute, until carrots are heated through.

Corn Custard

> *4 ears fresh corn**
> *½ cup water*
> *2 cups milk*
> *1 tablespoon butter or margarine*
> *3 eggs, well beaten*
> *½ teaspoon salt*
> *¼ teaspoon white pepper*
> *2 tablespoons chopped onion*
> *1 jar (2 ounces) chopped pimiento, drained*

Heat oven to 350°. Cut enough kernels from corn to measure 2 cups. Heat water to boiling; add corn. Heat to boiling; reduce heat. Cover and cook 9 to 10 minutes or until corn is tender; drain.

Heat milk and butter, stirring occasionally, until butter is melted. Mix all ingredients in ungreased 1½-quart casserole. Place casserole in rectangular pan, 13 × 9 × 2 inches, on oven rack. Pour very hot water into pan to depth of 1 inch. Bake about 45 minutes or until custard is firm and knife inserted in center comes out clean.

5 OR 6 SERVINGS

*2 cups frozen whole kernel corn, thawed, or 1 can (about 16 ounces) whole kernel corn, drained, can be substituted for the fresh corn. Do not cook.

Tangy Red Cabbage and Apples

1 medium head red cabbage (about 1½ pounds),
*   shredded (about 7½ cups)*
2 tablespoons white or cider vinegar
1 tablespoon vegetable oil
¼ cup sugar
2 tablespoons all-purpose flour
1 teaspoon salt
⅛ teaspoon pepper
½ cup water
¼ cup white or cider vinegar
2 medium all-purpose apples, cored and thinly
*   sliced*
1 small onion, sliced

Heat ½ inch salted water (¼ teaspoon salt, if desired, to 1 cup water) to boiling in Dutch oven; add cabbage and 2 tablespoons vinegar. Heat to boiling; reduce heat. Cover and simmer 5 to 8 minutes or until cabbage is crisp-tender; drain. Keep cabbage warm.

Heat vegetable oil in Dutch oven. Stir in sugar, flour, salt and pepper until blended. Stir in water, ¼ cup vinegar, the apples and onion. Cook over medium heat 3 to 5 minutes, stirring frequently, until apples are crisp-tender. Stir warm cabbage into sauce mixture.

6 SERVINGS

Microwave Directions. Mix ¼ cup water, 2 tablespoons vinegar and ½ teaspoon salt in 3-quart microwavable casserole until salt is dissolved; add cabbage. Cover tightly and microwave on high 8 to 9 minutes, stirring after 4 minutes, until cabbage is crisp-tender; drain. Keep cabbage warm.

Stir oil, sugar, flour, salt and pepper together in casserole until well blended. Stir in water, ¼ cup vinegar, the apples and onion. Microwave uncovered on high 4 to 5 minutes, stirring after 2 minutes, until sauce is thickened and apples are crisp-tender. Stir warm cabbage into sauce mixture.

Tangy Red Cabbage and Apples, Wilted Mixed Green Salad (page 105) and Stuffed Pork Tenderloin (page 46)

Sour Cream Cucumbers

½ cup white vinegar
½ cup water
1 tablespoon sugar
½ teaspoon salt
2 medium cucumbers, pared and cut
    into ⅛-inch slices
½ cup sour cream
⅛ teaspoon white pepper
1 tablespoon snipped fresh parsley

Mix vinegar, water, sugar and salt. Pour over cucumbers in glass or plastic bowl. Cover and refrigerate at least 2 but no longer than 24 hours; drain. Mix in sour cream and pepper; sprinkle with parsley. Serve immediately.

4 SERVINGS

Summer Succotash

Fresh corn and lima beans plus a rich touch of half-and-half elevate this humble classic to company fare. To keep the corn tender, cook it no longer than the 5 minutes called for. Succotash is derived from the native American *misickquatash*, dried corn and beans simmered in fat.

4 ears fresh corn*
2 cups shelled fresh lima beans (about
    3 pounds unshelled)*
⅓ cup cut-up lean salt pork or bacon
1 small onion, chopped (about ¼ cup)
½ cup half-and-half
¼ teaspoon salt
⅛ teaspoon pepper

Cut enough kernels from corn to measure 2 cups. Mix beans, salt pork and onion in 3-quart saucepan; add enough water to cover. Heat to boiling; reduce heat. Cover and simmer 20 to 25 minutes or until beans are tender. Stir in corn. Heat to boiling; reduce heat. Cover and simmer about 5 minutes or until corn is tender; drain. Stir in half-and-half, salt and pepper. Heat, stirring constantly, just until heated through.

6 SERVINGS

2 cups frozen whole kernel corn and 1 package (10 ounces) frozen baby lima beans can be substituted for the fresh corn and lima beans. Cook salt pork and onion in 3-quart saucepan over medium heat until salt pork is soft and onion is tender. Stir in beans and ¾ cup water. Heat to boiling; reduce heat. Cover and simmer 10 minutes. Stir in corn. Heat to boiling; reduce heat. Cover and simmer about 3 minutes or until corn and beans are tender; drain. Stir in half-and-half, salt and pepper. Heat, stirring constantly, just until heated through.

Oven-fried Eggplant

¼ cup butter or margarine
¾ cup dry bread crumbs
½ teaspoon salt
1 teaspoon snipped fresh or ¼ teaspoon
*   dried oregano*
¼ teaspoon garlic powder
¼ teaspoon pepper
1 medium eggplant (about 1½ pounds), pared
1 egg, slightly beaten
2 tablespoons milk

Heat oven to 375°. Heat butter in jelly roll pan, 15½ × 10½ × 1 inch, in oven until melted. Mix bread crumbs, salt, oregano, garlic powder and pepper in pie plate, 9 × 1¼ inches. Cut eggplant into ½-inch slices; cut large slices into halves. Mix egg and milk. Dip eggplant slices into egg mixture; coat with crumb mixture. Place in pan; turn each piece over to coat with butter. Bake uncovered 15 minutes; turn. Bake 15 minutes or until golden brown.

6 SERVINGS

Baked Honey Onions

3 large yellow onions (about 3 inches in diameter)
2 tablespoons butter or margarine
¼ cup honey
½ teaspoon ground allspice

Heat oven to 375°. Peel onions; cut crosswise into halves. Heat butter in square baking dish, 8 × 8 × 2 inches, in oven until melted; stir in honey and allspice. Arrange onions, cut sides down, in dish. Cover and bake about 1 hour or until tender. To serve, turn cut sides up and drizzle with honey mixture.

6 SERVINGS

Microwave Directions. Prepare as directed—except microwave butter in square microwave dish, 8 × 8 × 2 inches, on high 20 to 30 seconds or until butter is melted. Continue as directed—except cover with vented plastic wrap and microwave on high 8 to 10 minutes, rotating dish ½ turn after 5 minutes, until tender.

Baked Honey Onions and Meat Loaf (page 43)

Sweet Summer Peas

Fresh peas are incomparable in sweetness, flavor and texture to their canned cousins, although frozen peas are a close second in rank. In this French technique, the lettuce leaves that line the saucepan provide just enough moisture to steam the peas to delicate perfection.

3 large lettuce leaves
About 1½ pounds fresh green peas, shelled*
2 tablespoons thinly sliced green onion
    (with tops)
½ teaspoon snipped fresh or ⅛ teaspoon
    dried basil
1 tablespoon butter or margarine, softened

Line 1½-quart saucepan with lettuce. Spoon peas onto lettuce. Sprinkle with onion and basil; dot with butter. Cover and cook over low heat about 18 minutes or until peas are tender. Discard lettuce.

3 OR 4 SERVINGS

*1 package (10 ounces) frozen green peas, rinsed and drained, can be substituted for the fresh peas.

Microwave Directions. Line 1½-quart microwave casserole with lettuce. Spoon peas onto lettuce. Sprinkle with onions and basil; dot with butter. Cover tightly and microwave on high 7 to 9 minutes, stirring carefully after 4 minutes, until peas are tender. Let stand 3 minutes. Discard lettuce.

Baked Tomatoes with Horseradish Sauce

Softly whipped cream is a mellow counterpoint to prepared horseradish in the sauce for these crumb-topped tomatoes. This is delightful with roast beef and lamb and an unusual way to use summer's overabundance of ripe tomatoes. Tomatoes (or "love apples") were not common in American gardens until the mid-nineteenth century.

Horseradish Sauce (below)
3 large tomatoes, each cut into 4 slices
½ cup dry seasoned bread crumbs
2 tablespoons butter or margarine, melted

Heat oven to 425°. Prepare Horseradish Sauce. Place tomato slices in ungreased jelly roll pan, 15½ × 10½ × 1 inch. Mix bread crumbs and butter; sprinkle over tomatoes. Bake about 10 minutes or until tomatoes are hot and crumbs are golden brown. Serve with Horseradish Sauce.

6 SERVINGS

HORSERADISH SAUCE

½ cup whipping cream
3 tablespoons well-drained prepared horseradish
½ teaspoon salt

Beat whipping cream in chilled small bowl until soft peaks form. Fold in horseradish and salt.

Creamed Spinach

1½ pounds fresh spinach, coarsely chopped*
⅓ cup sour cream
¼ teaspoon salt
⅛ teaspoon ground nutmeg
Dash of pepper

Cover and cook spinach over medium heat with just the water that clings to leaves 5 to 8 minutes or until spinach is tender; drain thoroughly. Stir in remaining ingredients.

4 SERVINGS

*2 packages (10 ounces each) frozen chopped spinach, cooked and drained, can be substituted for the fresh spinach.

Microwave Directions. Place spinach with just the water that clings to leaves in 3-quart microwavable casserole. Cover tightly and microwave on high 6 to 8 minutes, stirring after 3 minutes, until spinach is tender. Stir in remaining ingredients.

Maple-baked Squash

3 pounds Hubbard or 2½ pounds butternut squash, pared and cubed*
¼ cup maple syrup
2 tablespoons butter or margarine
½ teaspoon salt
⅛ teaspoon pepper
3 slices bacon, crisply cooked and crumbled

Heat 1 inch salted water (¼ teaspoon salt, if desired, to 1 cup water) to boiling in 3-quart saucepan; add squash. Heat to boiling; reduce heat. Cover and boil gently 11 to 12 minutes or until squash is tender; drain.

Heat oven to 400°. Mash squash; stir in remaining ingredients except bacon. Turn mixture into ungreased 1-quart casserole. Bake uncovered 20 to 30 minutes or until hot. Sprinkle with bacon.

6 SERVINGS

*2 packages (12 ounces each) frozen cooked squash, thawed, can be substituted for fresh squash. Increase baking time to about 30 minutes. Stir before sprinkling with bacon.

Microwave Directions. Mix ¼ cup water and ¼ teaspoon salt in 1-quart microwavable casserole; add squash. Cover tightly and microwave on high 12 to 14 minutes, stirring after 5 minutes, until squash is tender; drain. Mash squash; stir in remaining ingredients except bacon. Cover and microwave 1 to 2 minutes or until hot; stir. Sprinkle with bacon.

Fried Apple Rings

Southern fried apples are a wonderful accompaniment to pork or ham. For best flavor, look for tart green cooking apples and leave them unpared. Fried bananas are a tropical variation that can be sprinkled with a few shreds of toasted coconut.

2 tablespoons butter or margarine
3 medium unpared cooking apples, cored and
cut into ½-inch slices
2 tablespoons packed brown sugar
¼ teaspoon ground cinnamon

Heat butter in 10-inch skillet until melted. Arrange apples in single layer in skillet. Cover and cook over medium-low heat 5 to 7 minutes, turning occasionally, until apples just begin to soften. Sprinkle with brown sugar and cinnamon. Cook 4 to 6 minutes, turning occasionally, until apples are of desired softness.

6 SERVINGS

Fried Bananas. Substitute 3 large ripe but firm bananas for the apples. Cut bananas crosswise into halves, then lengthwise into halves. Heat butter, brown sugar and cinnamon over medium-low heat, stirring constantly, until melted and bubbly. Arrange bananas in single layer in skillet. Cook uncovered 3 to 4 minutes, turning occasionally, until bananas are soft.

Broiled Honey Grapefruit

2 grapefruits, cut into halves
¼ cup honey
8 to 10 drops aromatic bitters or ½ teaspoon
lemon juice, if desired

Remove seeds from grapefruit halves. Cut around edges and sections to loosen; remove centers. Mix honey and bitters; spoon about 1 tablespoon honey mixture over each grapefruit half.

Set oven control to broil. Broil grapefruit halves with tops 5 inches from heat about 5 minutes.

4 SERVINGS

Luncheon Rice Salad

1 can (15¼ ounces) crushed pineapple, drained
1 cup chilled cooked rice
⅓ cup flaked coconut
¼ cup golden raisins
½ cup whipping cream
2 tablespoons sugar
½ teaspoon vanilla
½ teaspoon almond extract
¼ teaspoon ground ginger
Dash of salt
4 tablespoons slivered almonds
Salad greens

Mix pineapple, rice, coconut and raisins in medium bowl. Beat whipping cream, sugar, vanilla, almond extract, ginger and salt in chilled small bowl until stiff; fold into rice mixture. Stir in 3 tablespoons of the almonds. Spoon onto salad greens; garnish with 1 tablespoon slivered almonds.

4 TO 6 SERVINGS

Layered Carrot Mold

The turn of the century saw the phenomenal commercial success of packaged gelatin. With the advent of reliable refrigerators, the gelatin salad became an American mainstay. To preserve its layered look, the mold must be made in two stages. Do not substitute fresh pineapple for the canned variety; it will prevent the gelatin from setting.

> *1 cup boiling water*
> *1 package (3 ounces) orange-flavored gelatin*
> *1 cup cold water*
> *1 tablespoon lemon juice*
> *1 medium carrot, shredded (about 1 cup)*
> *1 cup boiling water*
> *1 package (3 ounces) orange-flavored gelatin*
> *1 package (3 ounces) cream cheese, softened*
> *½ cup cold water*
> *1 can (8 ounces) crushed pineapple in juice, undrained*

Pour 1 cup boiling water on 1 package gelatin in small bowl; stir until gelatin is dissolved. Stir in 1 cup cold water and the lemon juice. Refrigerate until slightly thickened; stir in carrot. Pour into 6 cup mold. Refrigerate about 1½ hours or until firm.

Pour 1 cup boiling water on 1 package gelatin in small bowl; stir until gelatin is dissolved. Beat gelatin gradually into cream cheese in medium bowl until smooth. Stir in ½ cup cold water and the pineapple; pour over carrot mixture. Refrigerate until firm; unmold. Garnish with salad greens if desired.

12 SERVINGS

Cranberry-Orange Mold

> *1 can (11 ounces) mandarin orange segments, drained (reserve juice)*
> *1 package (3 ounces) orange-flavored gelatin*
> *1 can (16 ounces) whole berry cranberry sauce*

Add enough water to reserved juice to measure 1¼ cups. Heat to boiling. Pour boiling mixture on gelatin in medium bowl; stir until gelatin is dissolved. Stir in cranberry sauce until sauce is melted. Stir in orange segments. Pour into 4-cup mold. Refrigerate at least 4 hours or until firm; unmold. Serve on salad greens if desired.

8 SERVINGS

Ambrosia Fruit Salad

Although myriad variations exist, this heavenly salad or dessert always contains oranges and coconut. It is best served icy cold. Ambrosia was the food of the Greek gods.

> *1 large grapefruit, pared and sectioned*
> *3 medium oranges, pared and sectioned*
> *½ cup seedless green grape halves*
> *1 to 2 tablespoons light corn syrup*
> *1 tablespoon dry sherry, if desired*
> *1 large banana, sliced*
> *¼ cup flaked coconut*

Cut grapefruit sections into halves. Mix grapefruit, oranges, grapes, corn syrup and sherry. Cover and refrigerate at least 2 hours but no longer than 24 hours. Stir in banana and coconut just before serving.

6 SERVINGS

Coleslaw

Opinion seems to be divided on the perfect coleslaw. One side favors using a tangy, vinegar-based dressing. The opposition prefers tossing the cabbage with a creamy mixture. Our version uses a cooked dressing with sour cream that can even be made in the microwave. "Coleslaw" comes from the Dutch *cool* for cabbage (*Kohl* in German) and *sla* for salad.

> *3 tablespoons sugar*
> *2 tablespoons all-purpose flour*
> *1 teaspoon dry mustard*
> *½ teaspoon salt*
> *⅛ teaspoon ground red pepper*
> *1 egg*
> *¾ cup water*
> *¼ cup lemon juice*
> *1 tablespoon butter or margarine*
> *½ cup sour cream*
> *1 pound green cabbage, shredded or finely chopped, (about 5 cups)*
> *1 medium carrot, shredded (about 1 cup)*
> *½ medium green bell pepper, finely chopped*

Mix sugar, flour, mustard, salt and red pepper in heavy 1-quart saucepan; beat in egg. Stir in water and lemon juice gradually until well blended. Cook over low heat 13 to 15 minutes, stirring constantly, until thick and smooth; remove from heat. Stir in butter until melted. Place plastic wrap directly on surface of dressing; refrigerate about 2 hours or until cool. Stir in sour cream.

Mix dressing, cabbage, carrot and bell pepper; toss well. Refrigerate at least 1 hour but no longer than 24 hours.

8 SERVINGS

Microwave Directions. Mix sugar, flour, mustard, salt and red pepper in 1-quart microwavable casserole. Decrease water to ⅔ cup. Stir in water and lemon juice gradually until well blended. Microwave uncovered on high 2 to 3 minutes, stirring every minute, until thickened.

Beat egg with hand beater until well blended. Stir about half of the hot mixture vigorously into beaten egg. Pour mixture into casserole, stirring until well blended. Microwave uncovered on medium-high (70%) 1½ to 2 minutes, stirring after 1 minute, until thick and smooth. Stir in butter until melted. Continue as directed.

Lettuce Wedges with Creamy Topping

> *1 medium head iceberg lettuce*
> *1 package (3 ounces) cream cheese, softened*
> *1 small carrot, grated (about ¼ cup)*
> *½ cup sour cream*
> *2 tablespoons finely chopped green bell pepper*
> *2 tablespoons shredded Cheddar cheese*
> *1 teaspoon lemon juice*
> *½ teaspoon salt*
> *¼ teaspoon onion salt*
> *Paprika*

Cut lettuce into 6 wedges. Place 1 lettuce wedge on each of 6 salad plates. Make 3 or 4 vertical cuts almost to bottom of each wedge if desired. Mix remaining ingredients except paprika; spoon onto wedges. Sprinkle with paprika.

6 SERVINGS

Wilted Mixed Green Salad

*8 cups bite-size pieces salad greens (spinach,
    red leaf lettuce, Boston lettuce, romaine)*
¼ cup white or cider vinegar
2 teaspoons sugar
½ teaspoon salt
*1½ teaspoons snipped fresh or ½ teaspoon dried
    dill weed*
½ teaspoon dry mustard
Dash of pepper
2 tablespoons water
1 tablespoon vegetable oil
2 slices bacon, crisply cooked and crumbled

Place greens in salad bowl. Heat remaining ingredients except bacon to boiling. Pour over greens and toss. Sprinkle with bacon.

8 SERVINGS

Microwave Directions. Decrease vinegar to 3 tablespoons. Heat all ingredients except greens and bacon uncovered to boiling in 2-cup microwavable measure. Continue as directed.

Potato Salad

2 pounds potatoes (about 6 medium), pared
1½ cups mayonnaise or salad dressing
1 tablespoon white or cider vinegar
1 tablespoon prepared mustard
1 teaspoon salt
¼ teaspoon pepper
2 medium stalks celery, chopped (about 1 cup)
1 medium onion, chopped (about ½ cup)
4 hard-cooked eggs, chopped

Heat 1 inch salted water (¼ teaspoon salt, if desired, to 1 cup water) to boiling; add potatoes. Cover and

heat to boiling; reduce heat. Cook 30 to 35 minutes or until potatoes are tender; drain. Cool slightly; cut into cubes (about 6 cups).

Mix mayonnaise, vinegar, mustard, salt and pepper in 4-quart glass or plastic bowl. Add potatoes, celery and onion; toss. Stir in eggs. Cover and refrigerate at least 4 hours.

10 SERVINGS

Mixed Bean Salad

1 can (16 ounces) cut green beans, drained
1 can (16 ounces) kidney beans, drained
1 can (15 ounces) garbanzo beans, drained
1 can (2¼ ounces) sliced ripe olives, drained
¼ cup snipped fresh parsley
1 cup vegetable oil
¼ cup white or cider vinegar
2 tablespoons finely chopped onion
*1 tablespoon snipped fresh or 1 teaspoon
    dried basil*
*1½ teaspoons snipped fresh or ½ teaspoon
    dried oregano*
1 teaspoon sugar
1 teaspoon dry mustard
¾ teaspoon salt
¼ teaspoon pepper
2 cloves garlic, crushed

Mix beans, olives and parsley in large bowl. Shake remaining ingredients in tightly covered container; pour over beans. Cover and refrigerate, stirring occasionally, at least 3 hours but no longer than 24 hours. To serve, remove salad with slotted spoon.

6 SERVINGS

Mixed Bean Salad

Chapter 7

BISCUITS, MUFFINS AND QUICK BREADS

Many biscuits, muffins and quick breads have one ingredient in common: baking powder. Baking powder, a combination of baking soda ("saleratus") and cream of tartar, was first produced commercially in the 1850s. It single-handedly raises baked goods, then maintains their height. Before baking powder, cooks relied on either a beaten egg or baking soda for a light crumb in their baked goods. Sometimes egg wasn't enough, and an overdose of baking soda would leave an unpleasant alkaline taste.

Muffins were known to the English as "tea cakes," but we prefer them for breakfast, preferably hot with lots of good, yellow butter and jam. Muffins may get their name from "muffineer," an English device for shaking sugar over small cakes.

Quick breads, unlike yeast breads, require neither kneading nor rising. Made from easy batters, they can usually be assembled and baked in less than 1½ hours. It is best, however, to hold off slicing them until the second day, as they will hold together more successfully.

Cornmeal Biscuits (page 108), Butter-dipped Biscuits (page 108) and Strawberry Jam (page 237)

Cornmeal Biscuits

Biscuits are at their best when they're served piping hot from the oven. To make sure they reach the table that way, serve them in a napkin-lined basket. Serve with butter, homemade jam or honey.

½ cup firm butter or margarine
1½ cups all-purpose flour
½ cup yellow cornmeal
3 teaspoons baking powder
2 teaspoons sugar
½ teaspoon salt
¾ cup milk
Yellow cornmeal

Heat oven to 450°. Cut butter into flour, cornmeal, baking powder, sugar and salt with pastry blender until mixture resembles fine crumbs. Stir in milk until dough leaves side of bowl (dough will be soft and sticky). Turn dough onto lightly floured surface. Knead lightly 10 times. Roll or pat ½ inch thick. Cut with floured 2½-inch round cutter. Place on ungreased cookie sheet about 1 inch apart for crusty sides, touching for soft sides. Sprinkle cornmeal lightly over biscuits. Bake 12 to 14 minutes or until golden brown. Remove from cookie sheet immediately.

ABOUT 1 DOZEN BISCUITS

Butter-dipped Biscuits

Butter bakes into these biscuits, leaving them tender and rich-tasting. To save time and minimize cleanup, the butter is melted right in the baking pan.

¼ cup butter or margarine
1¼ cups all-purpose flour
2 teaspoons sugar
2 teaspoons baking powder
½ teaspoon salt
⅔ cup milk

Heat oven to 450°. Heat butter in square pan, 9 × 9 × 2 inches, in oven until melted. Mix flour, sugar, baking powder and salt in medium bowl. Add milk; stir with fork just until soft dough forms, about 30 strokes. Turn dough onto well-floured cloth-covered board. Coat dough lightly with flour. Knead lightly about 10 times. Roll or pat into 8-inch square. With floured knife, cut dough into halves, then cut each half into 9 strips. Dip each strip into melted butter, coating both sides. Arrange strips close together in 2 rows in pan. Bake 15 to 20 minutes or until golden brown.

18 BISCUITS

Sour Cream Biscuits

The development in 1930 of Bisquick®, the first baking mix, revolutionized home baking, making it possible to whip up a batch of biscuits, muffins and the like in the time it takes to preheat the oven. This ease of preparation is exemplified in these biscuits, which use only the mix and sour cream. For a savory touch, toss a handful of snipped chives into the biscuit mix before adding the sour cream.

2 cups baking mix
1 cup dairy sour cream

Heat oven to 450°. Mix baking mix and sour cream until dough forms. Turn dough onto cloth-covered board well dusted with baking mix. Roll gently in baking mix to coat; shape into ball. Knead 5 times. Roll or pat ½ inch thick. Cut with 1¾-inch round cutter dipped into baking mix.* Place on ungreased cookie sheet. Bake 8 to 10 minutes or until golden brown.

ABOUT 2 DOZEN BISCUITS

*Biscuits can be covered and refrigerated up to 2 hours. Bake as directed.

Date-Bran Muffins

Part of the dates in this recipe are blended right into the batter, giving the muffins their sweet flavor and dark, rich color. The remaining chopped dates punctuate the muffin in chewy nuggets.

½ cup hot water
¼ cup cut-up dates
1½ cups wheat bran
1 cup whole wheat flour
1 teaspoon baking powder
½ teaspoon baking soda
½ teaspoon salt
⅓ cup vegetable oil
1 egg
1 cup buttermilk
½ cup cut-up dates

Heat oven to 400°. Pour hot water over ¼ cup dates; reserve. Grease bottoms only of 12 medium muffin cups, 2½ × 1¼ inches. Mix bran, flour, baking powder, baking soda and salt. Place reserved date mixture, oil and egg in blender container. Cover and blend on medium speed about 1 minute or until smooth. Mix date mixture, buttermilk and bran mixture just until flour is moistened (batter will be lumpy). Stir in ½ cup dates gently. Divide batter evenly among muffin cups. Bake 20 to 22 minutes or until wooden pick inserted in center comes out clean.

1 DOZEN MUFFINS

Blueberry Muffins

2 cups all-purpose flour
½ cup sugar
2 teaspoons baking powder
½ teaspoon salt
¼ teaspoon ground cinnamon
¾ cup milk
½ cup butter or margarine, melted
½ teaspoon vanilla
1 egg, slightly beaten
1 cup fresh or frozen (thawed and drained) blueberries
1 tablespoon sugar

Heat oven to 400°. Grease bottoms only of 12 medium muffin cups, 2½ × 1¼ inches, or line with paper baking cups. Mix flour, ½ cup sugar, the baking powder, salt and cinnamon in large bowl. Stir in milk, butter, vanilla and egg just until blended. Fold in blueberries (batter will be lumpy). Divide batter evenly among muffins cups. Sprinkle each muffin with ¼ teaspoon sugar. Bake 25 to 30 minutes or until golden brown. Cool 5 minutes; remove from pan.

1 DOZEN MUFFINS

Banana Gems

1 egg
2 cups baking mix
⅓ cup sugar
1¼ cups mashed ripe bananas (about 3 medium)
3 tablespoons vegetable oil
Thin Icing (below)

Heat oven to 400°. Grease bottoms only of 48 small muffin cups, 1¾ × 1 inch, or 12 medium muffin cups, 2½ × 1¼ inches, or line with paper baking cups. Beat egg slightly; stir in remaining ingredients except Thin Icing just until moistened. Divide batter evenly among muffin cups. Bake small muffins 10 to 12 minutes, medium muffins 15 to 20 minutes or until golden brown. Remove from pan immediately; frost with Thin Icing. Serve warm.

4 DOZEN SMALL MUFFINS OR 1 DOZEN MEDIUM MUFFINS

THIN ICING

½ cup powdered sugar
2 to 3 teaspoons water

Mix powdered sugar and water until smooth and spreadable.

Herb Popovers

2 eggs
1 cup all-purpose flour
1 cup milk
½ teaspoon salt
¼ teaspoon ground sage
¼ teaspoon freshly ground pepper

Heat oven to 450°. Grease six 6-ounce custard cups generously. Beat eggs slightly; beat in remaining ingredients with hand beater just until smooth (do not overbeat). Fill custard cups about ½ full. Bake 15 minutes. Reduce oven temperature to 350°; bake 25 minutes longer or until golden brown. Remove from cups immediately; serve hot.

6 POPOVERS

French Breakfast Puffs

The recipe for these sweet buns was first published in the 1920s on Washburn-Crosby flour recipe cards. The recipe came from Miss Esoline Beauregard in Florida, who sent it to Washburn-Crosby urging them to try her mother's recipe.

⅓ cup shortening
½ cup sugar
1 egg
1½ cups all-purpose flour
1½ teaspoons baking powder
½ teaspoon salt
¼ teaspoon ground nutmeg
½ cup milk
½ cup sugar
1 teaspoon ground cinnamon
½ cup butter or margarine, melted

Heat oven to 350°. Grease 15 medium muffin cups, 2½ × 1¼ inches. Mix shortening, ½ cup sugar and egg thoroughly. Mix flour, baking powder, salt and nutmeg; stir into egg mixture alternately with milk. Fill muffin cups ⅔ full. Bake 20 to 25 minutes or until golden brown. Mix ½ cup sugar and cinnamon. Roll hot muffins immediately in melted butter, then in sugar-cinnamon mixture. Serve hot.

15 PUFFS

French Breakfast Puffs and Fried Apple Rings (page 99)

Bacon Corn Bread

1½ cups yellow cornmeal
½ cup all-purpose flour
¼ cup shortening or bacon fat
1½ cups buttermilk
2 teaspoons baking powder
1 teaspoon sugar
½ teaspoon salt
½ teaspoon baking soda
4 slices crisply cooked bacon, crumbled
2 eggs

Heat oven to 450°. Grease round pan, 9 × 1½ inches, or square pan, 8 × 8 × 2 inches. Mix all ingredients; beat vigorously 30 seconds. Pour into pan. Bake 25 to 30 minutes or until golden brown. Serve warm.

12 SERVINGS

Bacon Corn Sticks. Fill 18 greased corn stick pans about ⅞ full. Bake 12 to 15 minutes.

Corn Fritters

Vegetable oil
1 cup all-purpose flour
½ cup milk
1 teaspoon baking powder
1 teaspoon salt
1 teaspoon vegetable oil
2 eggs
1 can (16 ounces) whole kernel corn, drained

Heat oil (3 to 4 inches) in Dutch oven to 375°. Mix remaining ingredients except corn with hand beater until smooth. Stir in corn. Drop by rounded table-spoonfuls into hot oil. Fry about 5 minutes or until deep golden brown; drain on paper towels. Serve with maple syrup if desired.

6 TO 8 SERVINGS

Hush Puppies

The supposed origin of these fried corn cakes is well known: In an attempt to appease their hungry hounds as the evening's fish was being fried, hunters threw them bits of fried fish coating, yelling, "Hush, puppies!"

Vegetable oil
1 cup yellow or white cornmeal
½ cup all-purpose flour
¾ cup buttermilk
1 teaspoon baking powder
1 teaspoon salt
¼ teaspoon baking soda
2 tablespoons finely chopped onion
1 egg

Heat oil (1 inch) in Dutch oven to 375°. Mix remaining ingredients. Drop by rounded tablespoonfuls into hot oil. Fry about 3 minutes, turning once, until golden brown; drain on paper towels.

ABOUT 2 DOZEN HUSH PUPPIES

Quick Spoon Bread

The name says it all, a puddinglike bread that's soft enough to scoop up with a spoon. This recipe is extra easy; unlike some methods, it doesn't require presoaking the cornmeal in hot water. Spoonbread is porridge with egg beaten in, then baked until light and fluffy.

1 tablespoon butter or margarine
1 egg
¾ cup white cornmeal
½ teaspoon baking soda
½ teaspoon salt
1½ cups buttermilk

Heat oven to 400°. Heat butter in 1-quart casserole in oven until melted. Beat egg; stir in remaining ingredients. Pour into hot casserole. Bake 30 to 35 minutes or until knife inserted in center comes out clean. Serve hot and, if desired, with butter or gravy.

4 TO 6 SERVINGS

Cranberry-Orange Bread

Cranberry-Orange Bread is a Christmastime tradition for many. American settlers were introduced to the cranberry by natives of what is now the Cape Cod area. Quick breads always cut better the second day.

2 cups all-purpose flour
¾ cup sugar
1½ teaspoons baking powder
½ teaspoon salt
½ teaspoon baking soda
¼ cup butter or margarine, softened
1 tablespoon grated orange peel
¾ cup orange juice
1 egg
1 cup fresh or frozen (thawed and drained)
*   cranberries, chopped*
½ cup chopped nuts

Heat oven to 350°. Grease bottom only of loaf pan, 8½ × 4½ × 2½ or 9 × 5 × 3 inches. Mix flour, sugar, baking powder, salt and baking soda; stir in butter until mixture is crumbly. Stir in orange peel, orange juice and egg just until moistened; stir in cranberries and nuts. Spread in pan. Bake 8-inch loaf 1 hour 15 minutes, 9-inch loaf 55 to 65 minutes, or until wooden pick inserted in center comes out clean; cool 5 minutes. Loosen sides of loaf from pan; remove from pan. Cool completely before slicing.

1 LOAF

Easy Brown Bread

While most brown bread is a steamed batter of cornmeal, rye flour and whole wheat flour, this simplified version is baked in loaves that get their special texture from graham cracker crumbs. Moist and compact, the bread makes terrific tea sandwiches when spread with cream cheese.

2 cups graham cracker crumbs (about 26 squares)
1¾ cups all-purpose flour
2 teaspoons baking soda
½ teaspoon salt
1 cup golden raisins
¾ cup molasses
⅓ cup vegetable oil
2 eggs
2 cups buttermilk

Heat oven to 375°. Grease bottoms only of 2 loaf pans, 9 × 5 × 3 inches, or 3 loaf pans, 8½ × 4½ × 2½ inches. Mix crumbs, flour, baking soda, salt and raisins in large bowl. Mix molasses, oil and eggs in medium bowl; stir in buttermilk. Stir molasses mixture into crumb mixture until blended. Pour into pans. Bake 30 to 35 minutes or until wooden pick inserted in center comes out clean; cool 5 minutes. Loosen sides of loaves from pans; remove from pans. Cool completely before slicing.

2 OR 3 LOAVES

Country Nut Loaf with Cream Cheese Spread

2 cups all-purpose flour
1 cup chopped nuts, toasted
½ cup whole wheat flour
½ cup granulated sugar
½ cup packed brown sugar
1¼ cups milk
⅓ cup vegetable oil
3 teaspoons baking powder
½ teaspoon salt
2 eggs
Cream Cheese Spread (below)

Heat oven to 350°. Grease bottom only of loaf pan, 9 × 5 × 3 inches, or 2 loaf pans, 8½ × 4½ × 2½ inches. Mix all ingredients except Cream Cheese Spread; beat 30 seconds. Pour into pan. Bake 9-inch loaf 55 to 65 minutes, 8-inch loaves 55 to 60 minutes, or until wooden pick inserted in center comes out clean; cool 5 minutes. Loosen sides of loaf from pan; remove from pan. Cool completely before slicing. Serve with Cream Cheese Spread.

1 OR 2 LOAVES

CREAM CHEESE SPREAD

1 package (8 ounces) cream cheese, softened
¼ cup apricot or peach preserves

Beat cream cheese and preserves in small bowl on medium speed until fluffy. Cover and refrigerate.

Pumpkin Bread

2⅔ cups sugar
⅔ cup shortening
4 eggs
1 can (16 ounces) pumpkin (2 cups)
⅔ cup water
3⅓ cups all-purpose flour
2 teaspoons baking soda
1½ teaspoons salt
½ teaspoon baking powder
1 teaspoon ground cinnamon
1 teaspoon ground cloves
⅔ cup coarsely chopped nuts
⅔ cup raisins

Heat oven to 350°. Grease bottoms only of 2 loaf pans, 9 × 5 × 3 inches, or 3 loaf pans, 8½ × 4½ × 2½ inches. Mix sugar and shortening in large bowl. Mix in eggs, pumpkin and water. Blend in flour, baking soda, salt, baking powder, cinnamon and cloves. Stir in nuts and raisins. Pour into pans. Bake about 1 hour 10 minutes or until wooden pick inserted in center comes out clean; cool 5 minutes. Loosen sides of loaves from pans; remove from pans. Cool completely before slicing.

2 OR 3 LOAVES

Irish Soda Bread

3 tablespoons butter or margarine, softened
2½ cups all-purpose flour
2 tablespoons sugar
1 teaspoon baking soda
1 teaspoon baking powder
½ teaspoon salt
⅓ cup raisins, if desired
¾ cup buttermilk

Heat oven to 375°. Grease cookie sheet. Cut butter into flour, sugar, baking soda, baking powder and salt with pastry blender until mixture resembles fine crumbs. Stir in raisins and just enough buttermilk so that dough leaves side of bowl. Turn dough onto lightly floured surface. Knead 1 to 2 minutes or until smooth. Shape into round loaf, about 6½ inches in diameter. Place on cookie sheet. Cut an X shape about ½ inch deep through loaf with floured knife. Bake 35 to 45 minutes or until golden brown. Brush with softened butter or margarine, if desired.

1 LOAF

Blueberry Buckle Coffee Cake

A classic "buckle" is made by covering a layer of fruit with a cake batter and sweet crumbs. This coffee cake, made "buckle fashion," will buckle and crack as it bakes.

> 2 cups all-purpose flour
> ¾ cup sugar
> 2½ teaspoons baking powder
> ¾ teaspoon salt
> ¼ cup shortening
> ¾ cup milk
> 1 egg
> 2 cups fresh or frozen (thawed and drained) blueberries
> Crumb Topping (below)
> Glaze (right)

Heat oven to 375°. Grease square pan, 9 × 9 × 2 inches, or round pan, 9 × 1½ inches. Blend flour, sugar, baking powder, salt, shortening, milk and egg; beat 30 seconds. Carefully stir in blueberries. Spread batter in pan; sprinkle with Crumb Topping. Bake 45 to 50 minutes or until wooden pick inserted in center comes out clean. Drizzle with Glaze. Serve warm.

9 SERVINGS

CRUMB TOPPING

> ½ cup sugar
> ⅓ cup all-purpose flour
> ½ teaspoon ground cinnamon
> ¼ cup butter or margarine, softened

Mix all ingredients until crumbly.

GLAZE

> ½ cup powdered sugar
> ¼ teaspoon vanilla
> 1½ to 2 teaspoons hot water

Mix all ingredients until drizzling consistency.

New Orleans French Toast

What better place to have *real* French toast than New Orleans, the city that called French cuisine its own. Known in French as *pain perdu*, or lost bread, the recipe frugally uses stale bread to a delicious end. Serve with the maple syrup suggested, or top with fresh orange sections tossed with sugar and orange liqueur.

> ⅔ cup milk
> 1 tablespoon powdered sugar
> ¼ teaspoon salt
> 1 teaspoon grated orange peel
> 3 eggs
> 2 tablespoons butter or margarine
> 8 slices day-old bread

Beat all ingredients except butter and bread until smooth. Heat 1 tablespoon of the butter in 10-inch skillet over medium heat until melted. Dip several bread slices into egg mixture (stir egg mixture each time before dipping bread). Cook about 2 minutes on each side or until golden brown. Repeat with remaining bread slices, adding remaining butter as needed. Sprinkle with powdered sugar and serve with maple syrup if desired.

4 SERVINGS

Blueberry Buckle Coffee Cake

Old-time Coffee Cake

The spiced crumb topping for this walnut-studded cake is taken from the batter mixture before the liquid ingredients are added. A vanilla-scented glaze adds a final touch of sweetness. Like most coffee cakes, it's best eaten while still warm. If necessary, reheat it in a low oven for 10 to 15 minutes.

2¼ cups all-purpose flour
1¼ cups sugar
1 teaspoon salt
1 teaspoon baking soda
1 teaspoon ground cinnamon
1 teaspoon ground nutmeg
½ teaspoon ground cloves
½ teaspoon ground allspice
¾ cup firm butter or margarine
1 cup chopped walnuts
1 cup buttermilk
1 egg, slightly beaten
Glaze (right)

Heat oven to 375°. Grease square pan, 9 × 9 × 2 inches. Mix flour, sugar, salt, baking soda, cinnamon, nutmeg, cloves and allspice in large bowl. Cut in butter with pastry blender until mixture resembles fine crumbs; reserve 1 cup. Stir walnuts, buttermilk and egg into flour mixture just until moistened (batter will be thick and lumpy). Pour into pan; sprinkle with reserved crumb mixture. Bake 40 to 45 minutes or until wooden pick inserted in center comes out clean. Drizzle with Glaze. Serve warm.

9 SERVINGS

GLAZE

1 cup powdered sugar
2 tablespoons butter or margarine, melted
½ teaspoon vanilla
3 to 4 teaspoons hot water

Mix all ingredients until drizzling consistency.

Buttermilk Drop Doughnuts

Vegetable oil
2 cups all-purpose flour
¼ cup sugar
1 teaspoon salt
1 teaspoon baking powder
1 teaspoon ground nutmeg
½ teaspoon baking soda
¼ cup vegetable oil
¾ cup buttermilk
1 egg
Sugar or cinnamon sugar

Heat oil (2 to 3 inches) in Dutch oven to 375°. Mix flour, ¼ cup sugar, the salt, baking powder, nutmeg and baking soda in large bowl. Add oil, buttermilk and egg; beat with fork until smooth. Drop batter by teaspoonfuls (do not make too large or they will not cook through) into hot oil. Fry about 3 minutes or until golden brown on both sides; drain on paper towels. Immediately roll in sugar.

ABOUT 3½ DOZEN DROP DOUGHNUTS

Chapter 8

COFFEE CAKES, ROLLS AND YEAST BREADS

As good as bakery-made versions may be, there is nothing like the deep fragrance, crusty exterior and pillow-soft crumb of a homemade delicacy warm from the oven. Before yeast was available commercially in 1868, bakers grew it at home. Its strength varied greatly, so results were not uniform. Today's yeast is virtually foolproof and easy to use, whether you prefer the active dry granules or the cakes of fresh yeast found in refrigerated dairy cases.

If you think you don't have time to bake with yeast, think again. The prebaked dough for Brown and Serve Rolls can be kept on hand in the refrigerator or freezer. Batter breads require neither kneading nor shaping, and Quick Buttermilk Bread uses baking powder for fast preparation.

Breadmaking was central to American homemaking. In 1900, 95 percent of the flour sold in the United State was purchased for home baking. (That figure dropped to 15 percent by 1970.) Freshly baked bread was looked forward to with great anticipation, but nothing went to waste; turn-of-the-century housekeepers were advised to save old bread and dry rolls in an earthen crock for later use as crumbs.

Honey Twist Coffee Cake (page 130)

Raised Doughnuts

Introduced to the Americas by the Dutch, these sweet treats known as *olykoeks* (oily cakes) were originally fried in lard. Today, they are firmly established as the perfect companions to morning coffee. For a spiced version, add ground cinnamon, ginger and a pinch of nutmeg to the sugar before shaking the doughnuts.

5 cups all-purpose flour
½ cup sugar
1 teaspoon salt
2 packages active dry yeast
1¾ cups very warm milk (120° to 130°)
⅓ cup shortening
2 eggs
Vegetable oil
Sugar

Mix 2 cups of the flour, ½ cup sugar, salt and yeast in large bowl. Add milk, shortening and eggs. Beat on low speed 1 minute, scraping bowl frequently. Beat on medium speed 1 minute, scraping bowl frequently. Stir in remaining flour until smooth. Cover and let rise in warm place 50 to 60 minutes or until double. (Dough is ready if indentation remains when touched.)

Turn dough onto generously floured surface; roll around lightly to coat with flour. Flatten dough with hands or rolling pin to ½-inch thickness. Cut with floured doughnut cutter. Push together scraps and gently knead 2 or 3 times. Flatten dough to ½-inch thickness; cut with floured 3-inch doughnut cutter. Cover doughnuts and let rise 30 to 40 minutes or until double.

Heat oil (1½ to 2 inches) in Dutch oven to 350°. Slide doughnuts into hot oil with wide spatula. Fry about 1 minute on each side or until golden brown. Remove carefully from oil (do not prick surfaces); drain on paper towels. Roll or shake in sugar.

ABOUT 2 DOZEN DOUGHNUTS

No-knead Bran Rolls

3½ to 3¾ cups all-purpose flour
½ cup whole bran cereal
¼ cup packed brown sugar
1 teaspoon salt
1 package active dry yeast
1 cup very warm water (120° to 130°)
3 tablespoons shortening
1 egg

Mix 1¾ cups of the flour, the cereal, brown sugar, salt and yeast in large bowl. Add water, shortening and egg. Beat on low speed 1 minute, scraping bowl frequently. Beat on medium speed 1 minute, scraping bowl frequently. Stir in enough remaining flour, 1 cup at a time, to make dough easy to handle.

Place dough in greased bowl; turn greased side up. Cover and let rise in warm place about 1½ hours or until double. (Dough is ready if indentation remains when touched.)

Grease 2 round pans, 9 × 1½ inches. Punch down dough; divide into 24 equal pieces. With greased hands, shape each piece into a ball (dough will be slightly sticky). Place 12 balls in each pan. Cover and let rise about 45 minutes or until double.

Heat oven to 375°. Bake 20 to 25 minutes or until golden brown.

2 DOZEN ROLLS

Brown and Serve Rolls

Betty Crocker introduced the technique of partially baking rolls, then keeping them on reserve in the refrigerator or freezer, ready at a few moments' notice. The dough can be shaped into crusty round dinner rolls or brushed with butter and folded into Parker House rolls, named for the Parker House restaurant in Boston, which made them famous. Parker House Rolls appeared in *Miss Parloa's New Cook Book*, published by Washburn-Crosby in 1880.

4½ cups all-purpose flour
¼ cup sugar
1 teaspoon salt
1 package active dry yeast
¾ cup very warm water (120° to 130°)
¾ cup very warm milk (120° to 130°)
¼ cup shortening
Butter or margarine, softened

Mix 2 cups of the flour, the sugar, salt and yeast in large bowl. Add water, milk and shortening. Beat on low speed 1 minute, scraping bowl frequently. Beat on medium speed 1 minute, scraping bowl frequently. Stir in enough remaining flour, 1 cup at a time, to make dough easy to handle.

Turn dough onto lightly floured surface; knead about 5 minutes or until smooth and elastic. Place in greased bowl; turn greased side up. Cover and let rise in warm place about 1½ hours or until double. (Dough is ready if indentation remains when touched.)

Punch down dough; turn onto lightly floured surface. Shape into Dinner Rolls or Parker House Rolls as directed below. Brush with butter. Cover and let rise 35 to 40 minutes or until double.

Heat oven to 275°. Bake 20 to 30 minutes or until dry and set but not brown. Remove from pans and cool to room temperature. Place rolls in plastic bags, or wrap in plastic wrap (freezer-quality plastic) or aluminum foil. Store in refrigerator no longer than 8 days or freezer no longer than 2 months. To serve, heat oven to 400°. Heat rolls on ungreased cookie sheet 7 to 10 minutes or until brown and hot. (To serve immediately, heat oven to 400°. Bake 15 to 20 minutes or until golden brown.)

2 DOZEN ROLLS

Dinner Rolls. Grease 24 medium muffin cups, 2½ × 1¼ inches, or 2 cookie sheets. Divide dough into 24 equal pieces. Shape each piece into smooth ball. Place in muffin cups or about 3 inches apart on cookie sheets. Continue as directed above.

Parker House Rolls. Grease 2 square pans, 9 × 9 × 2 inches. Divide dough into halves. Flatten each half with hands or rolling pin into rectangle, 12 × 9 inches. Cut with floured 3-inch round cutter. Brush each circle with butter. Make crease across each circle; fold so top half slightly overlaps bottom half. Press edges together. Place close together in pans. Continue as directed above.

Squash Rolls

4½ to 5 cups all-purpose flour
½ cup sugar
1 teaspoon salt
1 package active dry yeast
1¼ cups very warm milk (120° to 130°)
1 cup mashed cooked winter squash*
2 tablespoons butter or margarine

Mix 2 cups of the flour, the sugar, salt and yeast in large bowl. Add milk, squash and butter. Beat on low speed 1 minute, scraping bowl frequently. Beat on medium speed 1 minute, scraping bowl frequently. Stir in enough remaining flour, 1 cup at a time, to make dough easy to handle.

Turn dough onto lightly floured surface; knead about 5 minutes or until smooth and elastic. Place in greased bowl; turn greased side up. Cover and let rise in warm place about 1½ hours or until double. (Dough is ready if indentation remains when touched.)

Grease 24 medium muffin cups, 2½ × 1¼ inches. Punch down dough; divide into 24 equal pieces. Shape each piece into 3 smooth balls. Place 3 balls in each muffin cup. Cover and let rise 30 to 45 minutes or until double.

Heat oven to 400°. Bake 15 to 20 minutes or until light brown.

2 DOZEN ROLLS

*1 cup frozen squash, thawed and brought to room temperature, can be substituted for the fresh squash.

Magic Balloon Buns

In this original Betty Crocker recipe, marshmallows are dipped in melted butter, then rolled in cinnamon sugar before being encased in a round of lightly sweetened dough. During baking, the marshmallow melts, leaving a cinnamon-flavored "balloon" in its wake.

2¼ to 2½ cups all-purpose flour
¼ cup sugar
½ teaspoon salt
1 package active dry yeast
½ cup very warm milk (120° to 130°)
¼ cup shortening
1 egg
1 cup sugar
1 tablespoon ground cinnamon
12 large marshmallows
⅓ cup butter or margarine, melted

Mix 1 cup of the flour, ¼ cup sugar, the salt and yeast in large bowl. Add milk, shortening and egg. Beat on

low speed 1 minute, scraping bowl frequently. Beat on medium speed 1 minute, scraping bowl frequently. Stir in enough remaining flour, 1 cup at a time, to make dough easy to handle.

Turn dough onto lightly floured surface; knead about 5 minutes or until smooth and elastic. Place in greased bowl; turn greased side up. Cover and let rise in warm place about 1½ hours or until double. (Dough is ready if indentation remains when touched.)

Grease 12 medium muffin cups, 2½ × 1¼ inches. Punch down dough; divide into 12 equal pieces. Flatten each piece with hands or rolling pin into 4-inch circle. Mix 1 cup sugar and the cinnamon in small bowl. Dip each marshmallow into melted butter, then into sugar-cinnamon mixture. Wrap circle of dough around each marshmallow, pinching bottom tightly. Dip into butter, then into sugar-cinnamon mixture. Place pinched side down in muffin cups. Cover and let rise about 30 minutes or until double.

Heat oven to 375°. Bake 25 to 30 minutes or until golden brown. Remove from pan immediately; cool slightly. Serve warm.

1 DOZEN BUNS

Country Oatmeal Bread

¾ cup boiling water
½ cup regular oats
3 tablespoons shortening
¼ cup light molasses
1 teaspoon salt
1 package active dry yeast
¼ cup warm water (105° to 115°)
1 egg
2¾ cups all-purpose flour
1 egg white, slightly beaten
¼ cup regular oats, crushed
¼ teaspoon salt

Grease loaf pan, 9 × 5 × 3 or 8½ × 4½ × 2½ inches. Combine boiling water, ½ cup oats, the shortening, molasses and 1 teaspoon salt in large bowl; cool to lukewarm. Dissolve yeast in warm water. Add yeast, egg and 1½ cups of the flour to the oat mixture. Beat on medium speed 2 minutes, scraping bowl frequently. Stir in remaining flour until smooth.

Smooth and pat batter in pan with floured hands; brush with egg white. Mix ¼ cup oats and ¼ teaspoon salt; sprinkle over top. Let rise in warm place about 1½ hours or until double.

Heat oven to 375°. Bake 50 to 55 minutes or until loaf is brown and sounds hollow when tapped. Remove from pan; cool on wire rack.

1 LOAF

Honey–Whole Wheat Bread (page 142)

Cinnamon Swirl Raisin Bread

Raisins are found in many of the world's most beloved breads, but Americans have a particular love for this sweet loaf rippled with cinnamon sugar. To top off the bread, drizzle the slightly cooled loaves with a thin glaze made from 1 cup powdered sugar, sifted, ¼ teaspoon vanilla and 1 to 2 tablespoons milk mixed until smooth.

> *6 to 6½ cups all-purpose flour*
> *½ cup sugar*
> *2 teaspoons salt*
> *2 packages active dry yeast*
> *2 cups very warm water (120° to 130°)*
> *¼ cup vegetable oil*
> *2 eggs*
> *1 cup raisins*
> *½ cup sugar*
> *1 tablespoon ground cinnamon*
> *Vegetable oil*
> *Butter or margarine, softened*

Mix 3 cups of the flour, ½ cup sugar, the salt and yeast in large bowl. Add water, ¼ cup oil and the eggs. Beat on low speed 1 minute, scraping bowl frequently. Beat on medium speed 1 minute, scraping bowl frequently. Stir in raisins and enough remaining flour, 1 cup at a time, to make dough easy to handle.

Turn dough onto lightly floured surface; knead 8 to 10 minutes or until smooth and elastic. Place in greased bowl; turn greased side up. Cover and let rise in warm place about 1 hour or until double. (Dough is ready if indentation remains when touched.)

Grease 2 loaf pans, 9 × 5 × 3 inches. Mix ½ cup sugar and the cinnamon. Punch down dough; divide into halves. Flatten each half with hands or rolling pin into rectangle, 18 × 9 inches. Brush with oil; sprinkle with half of the cinnamon mixture. Roll up tightly, beginning at 9-inch side. Press each end with side of hand to seal; fold ends under loaf. Place loaf, seam side down, in pan; brush with oil. Let rise about 1 hour or until double.

Heat oven to 375°. Bake 30 to 35 minutes or until loaves are deep golden brown and sound hollow when tapped. Remove from pans. Brush with butter; cool on wire rack.

2 LOAVES

Fresh Herb Batter Bread

Batter breads are quick and easy because they are neither kneaded nor shaped. The result is a moist, tender bread with a characteristically open texture. If the dough overrises, however, it will collapse. If it seems too high in the pan, remove it, punch it down and return it to the pan to rise again. Toasted, this herb bread is a delightful base for chicken salad sandwiches.

3 cups all-purpose flour
1 tablespoon sugar
1 teaspoon salt
1 package active dry yeast
1¼ cups very warm water (120° to 130°)
2 tablespoons snipped fresh parsley
2 tablespoons shortening
1½ teaspoons snipped fresh or ½ teaspoon
   dried rosemary
½ teaspoon snipped fresh or ¼ teaspoon
   dried thyme
Butter or margarine, softened

Mix 2 cups of the flour, the sugar, salt and yeast in large bowl. Add water, parsley, shortening, rosemary and thyme. Beat on low speed 1 minute, scraping bowl frequently. Beat on medium speed 1 minute, scraping bowl frequently. Stir in remaining flour until smooth. Scrape batter from side of bowl. Cover and let rise in warm place 35 to 40 minutes or until double.

Grease loaf pan, 9 × 5 × 3 inches. Stir down batter by beating about 25 strokes. Smooth and pat batter in loaf pan with floured hands. Cover and let rise about 30 minutes or until double. (Do not allow to overrise.)

Heat oven to 375°. Bake 40 to 45 minutes or until loaf sounds hollow when tapped. Brush top with butter. Remove loaf from pan; cool on wire rack.

1 LOAF

Rich Egg Braids

7¼ to 7½ cups all-purpose flour
¼ cup sugar
2 teaspoons salt
2 packages active dry yeast
2 cups very warm milk (120° to 130°)
¼ cup butter or margarine, softened
3 eggs
Butter or margarine, softened
2 tablespoons cold water
1 egg yolk

Mix 3 cups of the flour, the sugar, salt and yeast in large bowl. Add milk, ¼ cup butter and the eggs. Beat on low speed 1 minute, scraping bowl frequently. Beat on medium speed 1 minute, scraping bowl frequently. Stir in enough remaining flour, 1 cup at a time, to make dough easy to handle.

Turn dough onto lightly floured surface; knead about 5 minutes or until smooth and elastic. Place in greased bowl; turn greased side up. Cover and let rise in warm place 1 to 1½ hours or until double. (Dough is ready if indentation remains when touched.)

Grease large cookie sheet. Punch down dough; divide into thirds. Divide each third into 3 equal parts; shape each part into strand, about 14 inches long. Braid each group of 3 strands loosely on cookie sheet. Pinch ends and tuck under. Brush with butter. Cover and let rise 40 to 50 minutes or until double. Mix water and egg yolk; brush over braids.

Heat oven to 375°. Bake 25 to 30 minutes or until braids are golden brown and sound hollow when tapped. Remove braids from cookie sheet immediately; cool on wire rack.

3 BRAIDS

Chapter 9

PUDDINGS, CUSTARDS AND CREAMS

*P*uddings, custards and creams run the gamut from homey and filling to light and exquisitely elegant. Bread and rice puddings, fruit duffs and baked custards are rich in milk, eggs or both. Several come to the table right in the dishes in which they're baked, and second helpings are the rule rather than the exception.

For a sumptuous finish to a distinctive meal, present a regal Bavarian cream, Floating Islands or Nesselrode Pudding. These are the luxurious legacy of sophisticated desserts of past generations, harking to the days when elaborately molded creams and "jellies" reigned on dessert tables lit by candelabra. Pull your great-grandmother's pudding molds out from storage, or look for molds in antique shops and flea markets.

Caramel-Apple Bread Pudding (page 152)

Saucy Lemon Pudding Cake

This classic American dessert bakes into two layers, a creamy sauce on the bottom with a soft cake on top. As the dessert cools, the sauce thickens. This recipe is a relative of "cottage pudding," a square of moist cake served warm with a sauce, usually lemon.

2 eggs, separated
1 cup milk
1 teaspoon grated lemon peel
¼ cup lemon juice
1 cup sugar
¼ cup all-purpose flour
¼ teaspoon salt

Heat oven to 350°. Beat egg whites until stiff peaks form. Beat egg yolks slightly; beat in milk, lemon peel and lemon juice. Beat in remaining ingredients until smooth. Fold into beaten egg whites. Pour into ungreased 1-quart casserole. Place casserole in square pan, 9 × 9 × 2 inches, on oven rack; pour very hot water (1 inch deep) into pan.

Bake 45 to 50 minutes or until golden brown. Serve warm or cool, and if desired, with whipped cream. Refrigerate any remaining pudding cake immediately.

6 SERVINGS

Microwave Directions. Pour 1 cup very hot water into 1½-quart microwavable casserole in microwave oven. Place casserole of pudding mixture carefully in 1½-quart casserole. Microwave uncovered on medium-high (70%) 10 to 12 minutes or until wooden pick inserted in center comes out clean.

Vanilla Cream Pudding

½ cup sugar
2 tablespoons cornstarch
⅛ teaspoon salt
2 cups milk
2 egg yolks, slightly beaten
2 tablespoons butter or margarine, softened
2 teaspoons vanilla

Mix sugar, cornstarch and salt in 2-quart saucepan. Stir in milk gradually. Cook over medium heat, stirring constantly, until mixture thickens and boils. Boil and stir 1 minute. Stir at least half of the hot mixture gradually into egg yolks. Stir into hot mixture in saucepan. Boil and stir 1 minute; remove from heat. Stir in butter and vanilla. Pour into dessert dishes; serve warm or cool. Refrigerate any remaining pudding immediately.

4 SERVINGS

Chocolate Cream Pudding. Stir ⅓ cup cocoa into sugar mixture. Omit butter.

Coconut Cream Pudding. Stir ¾ cup flaked coconut in with the butter and vanilla.

Individual Baked Custards

Custard is at once comforting and elegant, the perfect ending to just about any meal. In the caramel variation, the hard caramel in the bottom of the custard cups melts into a clear amber sauce that trickles over the "cup custards'" when they are unmolded.

3 eggs, slightly beaten
⅓ cup sugar
1 teaspoon vanilla
Dash of salt
2½ cups milk, scalded
Ground nutmeg

Heat oven to 350°. Mix eggs, sugar, vanilla and salt in medium bowl. Stir in milk gradually. Pour into six 6-ounce custard cups; sprinkle with nutmeg. Place cups in rectangular pan, 13 × 9 × 2 inches, on oven rack. Pour very hot water into pan to within ½ inch of tops of cups.

Bake about 45 minutes or until knife inserted halfway between center and edge comes out clean. Remove cups from water. Serve warm or chilled. Refrigerate any remaining custards immediately.

6 SERVINGS

Caramel Custards. Before preparing custard, heat ½ cup sugar in heavy 1-quart saucepan over low heat, stirring constantly, until sugar is melted and golden brown. Divide among custard cups; tilt cups to coat bottoms. Allow to harden in cups about 10 minutes. Pour custard mixture over syrup. Bake as directed.

Unmold and serve warm, or if desired, refrigerate and unmold at serving time. Caramel syrup will run down sides of custard, forming a sauce.

Tapioca Cream

2 egg yolks, slightly beaten
2 cups milk
2 tablespoons sugar
2 tablespoons quick-cooking tapioca
¼ teaspoon salt
1 teaspoon vanilla
2 egg whites
¼ cup sugar
Whipping cream or whipped cream

Mix egg yolks, milk, 2 tablespoons sugar, the tapioca and salt in 2-quart saucepan. Cook over low heat, stirring constantly, until mixture boils; remove from heat. Cool 15 minutes. Press plastic wrap onto pudding; refrigerate until chilled. Stir in vanilla. Beat egg whites until foamy. Beat in ¼ cup sugar, 1 tablespoon at a time; continue beating until stiff and glossy. Fold into tapioca mixture. Spoon pudding into dessert dishes; serve with cream.

6 SERVINGS

Rice Chantilly with Lingonberry Sauce

½ cup sugar
1 envelope unflavored gelatin
¼ teaspoon salt
2 cups milk
4 egg yolks, slightly beaten
1 cup whipping cream
1 cup cooked rice
1 can (8½ ounces) crushed pineapple, drained,
   or ⅓ cup finely cut-up mixed candied fruit
1 teaspoon vanilla
Lingonberry Sauce (below)

Stir together sugar, gelatin and salt in 2-quart saucepan. Stir in milk and egg yolks gradually. Cook over medium heat, stirring constantly, just until mixture boils. (Do not boil or mixture will curdle.) Place pan in bowl of ice and water or refrigerate, stirring occasionally, just until mixture mounds slightly when dropped from a spoon.

Beat whipping cream in chilled bowl until stiff. Fold whipped cream, rice, pineapple and vanilla into gelatin mixture. Pour into 8 dessert dishes. Refrigerate about 2 hours or until chilled. Serve with Lingonberry Sauce. Refrigerate any remaining pudding immediately.

8 SERVINGS

LINGONBERRY SAUCE

1 container (16 ounces) water-packed
   lingonberries
1 cup sugar

Heat lingonberries and sugar to boiling, stirring constantly, until sugar is dissolved; reduce heat. Cook 5 minutes, stirring occasionally; cool.

Nesselrode Pudding

Created by a French chef in the nineteenth century, Nesselrode began as a frozen sweet, laden with chestnut purée, fruits and nuts, and flavored with maraschino liqueur. In America, it evolved into a molded dessert or pie. This version omits the traditional chestnut purée and highlights the chopped nuts, dried fruit and rum.

2 envelopes unflavored gelatin
½ cup cold water
4 eggs, separated
½ cup sugar
2 cups half-and-half
½ cup finely chopped almonds, toasted
½ cup finely chopped candied cherries
¼ cup finely chopped raisins
¼ cup finely chopped citron
2 tablespoons rum or 1 teaspoon rum extract
2 teaspoons vanilla
⅛ teaspoon salt

Sprinkle gelatin on cold water in small bowl to soften. Mix egg yolks and sugar in heavy 2-quart saucepan. Stir in half-and-half gradually; stir in gelatin. Cook over medium-low heat, stirring constantly, until mixture thickens; do not boil. Place pan in bowl of ice and water, or refrigerate 20 to 60 minutes, stirring occasionally, until mixture mounds when dropped from a spoon.

Mix almonds, cherries, raisins and citron thoroughly. Stir almond mixture, rum and vanilla into gelatin mixture. Beat egg whites and salt until stiff but not dry. Fold into almond-gelatin mixture. Pour into 6-cup mold. Refrigerate about 3 hours or until firm; unmold. Garnish with maraschino cherries if desired. Refrigerate any remaining pudding immediately.

12 SERVINGS

Strawberry Bavarian Cream

Usually Bavarian creams, custards lightened with whipped cream and bound with gelatin, are firm enough to unmold and serve with a sauce. This dainty version, pink with crushed berries, is poured directly into individual dessert dishes. Garnish with a pouf of whipped cream and a whole, perfect strawberry.

½ cup sugar
1 cup milk
1 envelope unflavored gelatin
2 eggs, separated
1 pint strawberries, mashed
¼ teaspoon cream of tartar
¼ cup sugar
½ cup whipping cream

Mix ½ cup sugar, the milk, and gelatin in 1½-quart saucepan. Beat egg yolks slightly; stir into gelatin mixture. Heat just to boiling over medium heat, stirring constantly; remove from heat. Stir in strawberries. Place pan in bowl of ice and water, or refrigerate about 30 minutes, stirring occasionally, until mixture mounds when dropped from a spoon.

Beat egg whites and cream of tartar in large bowl until foamy. Beat in ¼ cup sugar, 1 tablespoon at a time; continue beating until stiff and glossy. Do not underbeat. Fold gelatin mixture into egg whites.

Beat whipping cream in chilled medium bowl until stiff. Fold whipped cream into egg white mixture. Spoon carefully into 6 to 8 dessert dishes. Refrigerate about 2 hours or until chilled. Refrigerate any remaining pudding immediately.

6 TO 8 SERVINGS

Chocolate Bavarian Cream

½ cup sugar
3 tablespoons cocoa
1 envelope unflavored gelatin
2¼ cups milk
1 tablespoon butter or margarine
2 egg whites
½ teaspoon cream of tartar
1 cup whipping cream

Mix sugar, cocoa and gelatin in 2-quart saucepan. Stir in milk and butter. Cook over medium heat, stirring constantly, just until mixture boils (butter should be melted). Place pan in bowl of ice and water, or refrigerate, stirring occasionally, just until mixture mounds slightly when dropped from a spoon.

Beat egg whites and cream of tartar in large bowl until stiff. Fold gelatin mixture into egg whites. Beat whipping cream in chilled medium bowl until stiff. Fold whipped cream into egg white mixture. Spoon into sherbet glasses. Refrigerate about 2 hours or until chilled. Refrigerate any remaining pudding immediately.

8 SERVINGS

Microwave Directions. Mix sugar, cocoa and gelatin in 2-quart microwavable casserole. Stir in milk and butter gradually. Microwave uncovered on high 5 to 7 minutes or until boiling; stir until gelatin is dissolved. Continue as directed.

Chapter 10

PASTRIES, PIES AND COBBLERS

*D*eveloped by resourceful homemakers, pastries, pies and cobblers are the essence of American creativity. These desserts were enjoyed so often that families built special pie safes, covered cabinets constructed so air could circulate to cool the pies while they were protected from busy flies and other pests.

Desserts made with pastry and biscuit dough offer year 'round pleasure. The first rhubarb pie of spring is a harbinger of the bountiful months to come. As summer gets under way, peaches, cherries and blueberries are tucked under pastry lattices, crisp crumbs and mounds of dumplings. Autumn is for apple pie, of course, and apple pandowdy and apple dumplings. Pastry desserts in winter often feature dried fruits, nuts and chocolate.

"As American as apple pie" isn't an empty cliché. Our forebears happily ate pie for breakfast, pie for lunch and pie for supper.

Danish Puff (page 164) and Spicy Sugared Nuts (page 221)

Country Apple Pie

Pastry for 10-inch Two-Crust Pie (page 166)
1 cup sugar
¼ cup all-purpose flour
¾ teaspoon ground cinnamon
½ teaspoon ground nutmeg
Dash of salt
8 cups thinly sliced pared tart cooking apples
*   (about 8 medium)*
4 tablespoons whipping cream

Heat oven to 425°. Prepare pastry. Mix sugar, flour, cinnamon, nutmeg and salt. Stir in apples. Turn into pastry-lined deep-dish pie plate, 9 × 1½ inches, or pie plate, 10 × 1½ inches. Drizzle with 3 tablespoons of the whipping cream.

Cover with top crust that has slits cut in it; seal and flute. Brush with remaining whipping cream. Top with leaf or other shapes cut from pastry scraps if desired. Bake 40 to 45 minutes or until crust is brown and juice begins to bubble through slits in crust.

8 SERVINGS

Chocolate Cream Pie

9-inch Baked Pie Shell (page 166)
1½ cups sugar
⅓ cup cornstarch
½ teaspoon salt
2½ cups milk
2 ounces unsweetened chocolate, cut up
3 egg yolks, slightly beaten
1 tablespoon vanilla
Meringue (below)

Prepare Baked Pie Shell. Heat oven to 400°. Mix sugar, cornstarch and salt in 2-quart saucepan. Stir in milk gradually; add chocolate. Cook over medium heat, stirring constantly, until chocolate is melted and mixture thickens and boils. Boil and stir 1 minute. Stir at least half of the hot mixture gradually into egg yolks. Blend into hot mixture in saucepan. Boil and stir 1 minute; remove from heat. Stir in vanilla. Pour into pie shell.

Prepare Meringue; spoon onto hot pie filling. Spread over filling, carefully sealing meringue to edge of crust to prevent shrinking or weeping. Bake 8 to 12 minutes or until delicate brown. Cool pie away from draft. Refrigerate any remaining pie immediately.

8 SERVINGS

MERINGUE

3 egg whites
¼ teaspoon cream of tartar
6 tablespoons sugar
½ teaspoon vanilla

Beat egg whites and cream of tartar in 1½-quart bowl until foamy. Beat in sugar, 1 tablespoon at a time; continue beating until stiff and glossy. Do not underbeat. Beat in vanilla.

Lemon Cream Tarts

Baked Tart Shells (below)
2 tablespoons butter or margarine
2 tablespoons all-purpose flour
⅓ cup sugar
⅓ cup water
2 teaspoons grated lemon peel
2 tablespoons lemon juice
1½ cups whipping cream
1 to 2 drops yellow food color, if desired

Prepare Baked Tart Shells. Heat butter in 1-quart saucepan over low heat until melted. Stir in flour. Cook over low heat, stirring constantly, until mixture is smooth and bubbly; remove from heat. Stir in sugar, water, 1 teaspoon of the lemon peel and the lemon juice. Heat to boiling, stirring constantly. Boil and stir 1 minute. Cover and refrigerate about 1 hour or until chilled.

Beat whipping cream in chilled large bowl until stiff. Stir 2 spoonfuls whipped cream and food color into lemon mixture to soften it; fold into whipped cream. Divide filling among tart shells; sprinkle with remaining lemon peel. Garnish with mint leaves if desired. Cover and refrigerate any remaining tarts.

8 TARTS

BAKED TART SHELLS

Heat oven to 475°. Prepare pastry as directed for 9-inch One-Crust Pie (page 166)—except roll into 15-inch circle. Cut pastry into eight 4½-inch circles; fit over backs of medium muffin cups or 6-ounce custard cups, making pleats so pastry will fit closely. (If using individual pie pans or tart pans, cut pastry circles 1 inch larger than inverted pans; fit into pans.) Prick thoroughly with fork to prevent puffing. Place on cookie sheet. Bake 8 to 10 minutes or until light brown. Cool before removing from pans.

Apple Cider Brown Betty

In autumn, fresh cider and tart cooking apples are plentiful. Combine them in this layered dessert, made with graham cracker crumbs instead of the more usual bread crumbs. (A brown Betty is simply a pandowdy topped with crumbs.) Serve warm or at room temperature.

1 cup graham cracker crumbs (about 15 crackers)
½ cup packed brown sugar
1½ teaspoons ground cinnamon
¼ teaspoon ground nutmeg
¼ cup butter or margarine, melted
8 cups thinly sliced pared tart cooking apples (about 8 medium)
1 cup apple cider or juice

Heat oven to 350°. Mix cracker crumbs, brown sugar, cinnamon and nutmeg. Stir in butter until well blended. Sprinkle ⅔ cup of the crumb mixture in ungreased square pan, 9 × 9 × 2 inches; top with half of the apple slices. Repeat with ⅔ cup of the crumb mixture and remaining apple slices. Pour apple cider over apples; sprinkle with remaining crumb mixture. Bake uncovered 50 to 55 minutes or until apples are tender. Serve with cream if desired.

8 SERVINGS

Cherry Crisp

1 pound fresh dark sweet cherries, pitted*
⅔ cup packed brown sugar
½ cup all-purpose flour
½ cup regular oats
½ teaspoon ground cinnamon
¼ teaspoon ground nutmeg
⅓ cup butter or margarine, softened

Heat oven to 375°. Spread cherries in ungreased square pan, 8 × 8 × 2 inches. Mix remaining ingredients with fork. Sprinkle over cherries. Bake about 30 minutes or until topping is golden brown. Serve warm with cream or ice cream if desired.

6 SERVINGS

*2 cans (16 ounces each) pitted dark sweet cherries, drained, can be substituted for the fresh cherries.

Microwave Directions. Spread cherries in square microwavable dish, 8 × 8 × 2 inches. Microwave uncovered on high 7 to 10 minutes or until cherries are hot and bubbly. Let stand 10 minutes.

Fresh Peach Cobbler

The name "cobbler" probably came about because this fruit and biscuit dessert can be "cobbled up" (meaning "put together quickly"). For extra-efficient cobbling up, dip the peaches in boiling water for a mere 30 seconds, then immediately plunge them into ice water; the skins should peel right off. Use ripe, sweet peaches.

½ cup sugar
1 tablespoon cornstarch
¼ teaspoon ground nutmeg
4 cups peeled, sliced fresh peaches*
1 teaspoon lemon juice
1 cup all-purpose flour
1 tablespoon sugar
1½ teaspoons baking powder
½ teaspoon salt
3 tablespoons shortening
½ cup milk

Heat oven to 400°. Mix ½ cup sugar, the cornstarch and nutmeg in 2-quart saucepan. Stir in peaches and lemon juice. Cook over medium heat, stirring constantly, until mixture thickens and boils. Boil and stir 1 minute. Pour into ungreased 2-quart casserole. Stir together flour, 1 tablespoon sugar, the baking powder and salt. Add shortening and milk. Cut through shortening with fork until dough forms a ball. Drop mixture by 6 to 8 spoonfuls onto hot fruit. Bake 25 to 30 minutes or until topping is golden brown. Serve warm with cream or whipped cream if desired.

6 TO 8 SERVINGS

*2 packages (16 ounces each) frozen sliced peaches, thawed and well drained, can be substituted for the fresh peaches.

Peach-Custard Kuchen

German-style butter dough is an easily mixed base for this peaches-and-cream dessert. Sprinkled with cinnamon sugar, the peaches partially bake to release some of their juices before the custard is poured over them and the baking is completed.

1 cup all-purpose flour
2 tablespoons sugar
¼ teaspoon salt
⅛ teaspoon baking powder
¼ cup butter or margarine, softened
1½ cups sliced fresh peaches (about 3 medium)*
⅓ cup sugar
1 teaspoon ground cinnamon
2 egg yolks
1 cup whipping cream

Heat oven to 400°. Stir together flour, 2 tablespoons sugar, the salt and baking powder. Work in butter until mixture is crumbly. Pat mixture firmly and evenly in bottom and halfway up sides of ungreased square pan, 8 × 8 × 2 inches. Arrange peaches in pan. Mix ⅓ cup sugar and the cinnamon; sprinkle over peaches. Bake 15 minutes.

Blend egg yolks and whipping cream; pour over peaches. Bake 25 to 30 minutes or until custard is set and edges are light brown. Serve warm. Refrigerate any remaining dessert.

9 SERVINGS

*1 package (8 ounces) frozen sliced peaches, thawed and drained, or 1 can (16 ounces) sliced peaches, drained, can be substituted for the fresh peaches.

Peach-Custard Kuchen

Blueberry Grunt with Nutmeg Sauce

Grunts are made from hot fruit mixtures topped with mounds of biscuit dough, simmered, first uncovered, then covered, until the biscuits are cooked. It is said the dessert acquired its name because the biscuits "grunt" as they rise and collapse into the bubbling filling.

> *½ cup sugar*
> *2 tablespoons cornstarch*
> *½ cup water*
> *1 teaspoon lemon juice*
> *4 cups fresh blueberries**
> *1 cup all-purpose flour*
> *2 tablespoons sugar*
> *1½ teaspoons baking powder*
> *¼ teaspoon salt*
> *¼ teaspoon ground nutmeg*
> *¼ cup butter or margarine*
> *⅓ cup milk*
> *Nutmeg Sauce (right)*

Mix ½ cup sugar and the cornstarch in 3-quart saucepan. Stir in water and lemon juice until well blended. Stir in blueberries. Cook over medium heat, stirring constantly, until mixture thickens and boils. Boil and stir 1 minute.

Mix flour, 2 tablespoons sugar, the baking powder, salt and nutmeg. Cut in butter until mixture resembles fine crumbs. Stir in milk. Drop dough by 6 spoonfuls onto hot blueberry mixture. Cook uncovered over low heat 10 minutes; cover and cook 10 minutes longer. Serve hot with Nutmeg Sauce.

6 SERVINGS

NUTMEG SAUCE

> *¾ cup whipping cream*
> *1 egg, beaten until foamy*
> *2 tablespoons sugar*
> *½ teaspoon ground nutmeg*
> *2 tablespoons butter or margarine*

Heat all ingredients except butter over medium heat, stirring constantly, until mixture thickens and boils. Boil and stir 1 minute; remove from heat. Stir in butter until melted. Serve immediately or refrigerate.

*1 package (16 ounces) frozen blueberries can be substituted for the 4 cups fresh blueberries; do not thaw berries.

Microwave Directions. Prepare blueberry mixture in 3-quart microwavable casserole. Microwave uncovered on high 5 minutes; stir. Microwave uncovered on medium-high (70%) 4 to 6 minutes or until boiling; stir. Drop dough by 6 spoonfuls onto hot blueberry mixture. Microwave uncovered on medium-high (70%) 4 to 7 minutes or until top of dough is almost dry. Let stand uncovered 5 minutes before serving.

Prepare Nutmeg Sauce in 2-cup Microwavable measure. Microwave uncovered on medium-high (70%) 2 minutes 30 seconds to 3 minutes 30 seconds, briskly stirring with fork every minute, until thick. Stir in butter.

Apple Pandowdy

This hot fruit dessert, which first appeared on "American" tables in the seventeenth century, is a cross between a pudding and a pie. The pastry dough is baked in one piece on top of the fruit, then "dowdied" (cut up) and mixed into the filling before going back into the oven.

> ½ cup granulated sugar
> ½ cup packed brown sugar
> 1 teaspoon ground cinnamon
> ½ teaspoon ground nutmeg
> ¼ teaspoon salt
> 8 cups sliced pared tart cooking apples
>   (about 8 medium)
> 2 tablespoons butter or margarine
> Pastry for 9-inch One-Crust Pie (page 166)
> Whipping cream

Heat oven to 375°. Mix sugars, cinnamon, nutmeg and salt; stir in apples. Pour into ungreased 2-quart casserole; dot with butter. Prepare pastry as directed— except roll into shape to fit top of casserole. Cut slits near center; fit pastry inside rim of casserole. Bake 30 minutes; remove from oven. Cut crust into small pieces with sharp knife, mixing pieces into apple filling. Bake about 30 minutes or until apples are tender and pieces of crust are golden. Serve warm with cream.

9 SERVINGS

Chapter 11

CAKES AND DESSERTS

*I*n *the days before heat-regulated ovens, home bakers were offered all kinds of advice on how to tell if the oven was "quick" (hot) enough or too hot. One suggestion was to toss a small amount of flour onto the oven floor; if it burned, the oven was too hot, and if it didn't color after a few minutes, the oven was too cool. The Washburn-Crosby Co. Gold Medal Flour Cook Book (1910) proposed another test: "If a piece of white paper turns a deep yellow in five minutes the oven is right for butter cakes; if it turns a light yellow in five minutes it is ready for sponge cake."*

One early breakthrough for the home cake baker was the invention of the egg beater (patented in 1870). Until then, eggs were beaten with forks, variations on the whisk, even with wooden switches, for as long as twenty or thirty minutes, depending on the recipe. In 1943, Betty Crocker offered a new method in cake preparation that eliminated the need to cream the shortening and sugar first. Instead, sugar was sifted with the other dry ingredients, then the shortening was added. This reduced mixing time by as much as half. In 1961, presifted Gold Medal flour further streamlined cake making. Among all the improvement, there is one piece of advice that will never go out of date: Resist the temptation to open the oven door during the first half of the baking time. (Too many good cakes have suffered because of impatient bakers.)

Chocolate-Marshmallow Ribbon Cake (page 184)

Chocolate-Marshmallow Ribbon Cake

1 cup all-purpose flour
¼ cup cocoa
1 teaspoon baking powder
¼ teaspoon salt
3 eggs
1 cup granulated sugar
⅓ cup water
1 teaspoon vanilla
Powdered sugar
Marshmallow Frosting (right)
Chocolate Glaze (right)

Heat oven to 375°. Line jelly roll pan, 15½ × 10½ × 1 inch, with aluminum foil; grease generously. Mix flour, cocoa, baking powder and salt; reserve. Beat eggs in small bowl on high speed about 3 minutes or until very thick and lemon colored. Pour eggs into large bowl. Beat in granulated sugar gradually. Beat in water and vanilla on low speed. Beat in dry ingredients on low speed just until batter is smooth. Pour into pan, spreading batter to corners.

Bake 12 to 15 minutes or until top springs back when touched lightly. Loosen cake immediately from edges of pan; invert on towel generously sprinkled with powdered sugar. Remove foil carefully; cool cake completely.

Prepare Marshmallow Frosting. Cut cake crosswise into 4 rectangles, each about 10 × 3¾ inches. Put rectangles together with about ¾ cup frosting between layers; frost top with remaining frosting. Prepare Chocolate Glaze. Pour over cake, allowing some to drizzle down sides. Sprinkle with chopped toasted almonds if desired.

ABOUT **12** SERVINGS

MARSHMALLOW FROSTING

2 egg whites
1½ cups sugar
¼ teaspoon cream of tartar
1 tablespoon light corn syrup
⅓ cup water
10 large marshmallows, cut into fourths

Mix egg whites, sugar, cream of tartar, corn syrup and water in nonaluminum 3-quart saucepan. Cook over low heat, beating until stiff peaks form and scraping bottom and side of saucepan occasionally; remove from heat. Add marshmallows; beat until smooth.

CHOCOLATE GLAZE

1 ounce unsweetened chocolate
1 teaspoon butter or margarine
1 cup powdered sugar
5 teaspoons boiling water

Heat chocolate and butter over low heat until melted. Blend in powdered sugar and water until smooth. Stir in additional boiling water, ½ teaspoon at a time, until of drizzling consistency.

Jelly Roll

A versatile cake delicious with any number of fillings, the simplest being an even layer of jelly or jam. Since it is spread so thinly, the batter for a jelly roll requires very little baking time. It's important to remove the cake from the pan immediately after it comes out of the oven, so it will still be flexible enough to roll up. Cakes leavened with whipped eggs are known as "sponge" cakes.

1 cup cake flour or ¾ cup all-purpose flour
1 teaspoon baking powder
¼ teaspoon salt
3 eggs
1 cup granulated sugar
⅓ cup water
1 teaspoon vanilla
About ⅔ cup jelly or jam
Powdered sugar

Heat oven to 375°. Line jelly roll pan, 15½ × 10½ × 1 inch, with aluminum foil; grease generously. Mix flour, baking powder and salt; reserve. Beat eggs in small bowl on high speed about 3 minutes or until very thick and lemon colored. Pour eggs into large bowl. Beat in granulated sugar gradually. Beat in water and vanilla on low speed. Beat in dry ingredients on low speed just until batter is smooth. Pour into pan, spreading batter to corners.

Bake 12 to 15 minutes or until wooden pick inserted in center comes out clean. Loosen cake immediately from edges of pan; invert on towel generously sprinkled with powdered sugar. Remove foil carefully. Trim off stiff edges of cake if necessary (to prevent cake from splitting when rolled).

While it is hot, carefully roll cake and towel from narrow end. Cool on wire rack at least 30 minutes. Unroll cake and remove towel. Beat jelly with fork just enough to soften; spread over cake. Roll up; sprinkle with powdered sugar.

10 SERVINGS

Ice-Cream Roll. Omit jelly and powdered sugar. Soften 1 pint strawberry, chocolate or peppermint ice cream slightly. Spread over unrolled cake; roll up carefully. Place seam side down on piece of aluminum foil, 18 × 12 inches. Wrap; freeze about 4 hours or until firm. Remove from freezer about 15 minutes before serving.

Strawberry-Cream Roll. Omit jelly and powdered sugar. Beat ½ cup whipping cream and 2 tablespoons powdered sugar in chilled bowl until stiff. Spread over unrolled cake. Sprinkle 2 cups sliced strawberries over whipped cream; roll up carefully. Refrigerate until serving time. Garnish with sliced strawberries and serve with additional sweetened whipped cream if desired.

Gold and Silver Angel Food Cake with Lemon Glaze

Originally called Angel's Food when it was invented in St. Louis, Missouri, in the 1880s, this tube cake usually has a pristine white crumb, since it is traditionally made with neither butter nor egg yolks. In this marbleized version, egg yolks are folded into half of the batter; the resulting gold batter is then swirled with the plain batter. To retain its fluffy texture, cool the cake upside down over a bottle or funnel to minimize shrinking. When serving, separate slices with two forks (or use a serrated knife).

> *1 cup cake flour*
> *1½ cups powdered sugar*
> *1½ cups egg whites (about 12)*
> *1½ teaspoons cream of tartar*
> *¼ teaspoon salt*
> *1 cup granulated sugar*
> *4 egg yolks*
> *1 teaspoon lemon extract*
> *1 to 2 drops yellow food color, if desired*
> *1 teaspoon vanilla*
> *Lemon Glaze (right)*

Heat oven to 375°. Mix flour and powdered sugar; reserve. Beat egg whites, cream of tartar and salt in large bowl until foamy. Beat in granulated sugar, 2 tablespoons at a time, on high speed until stiff peaks form. Beat egg yolks, lemon extract and food color in small bowl about 5 minutes or until very thick and lemon colored. Fold vanilla into egg whites.

Sprinkle flour-sugar mixture, ¼ cup at a time, over egg whites, folding in gently just until flour-sugar mixture disappears. Pour half of the batter into another bowl; fold in egg yolks gently. Spoon yellow and white batters alternately into ungreased tube pan. 10 × 4 inches. Cut through batters gently to swirl.

Bake 30 to 35 minutes or until top springs back when touched lightly. Invert pan on heatproof funnel or bottle immediately until cake is completely cool. Remove from pan. Prepare Lemon Glaze; spread over top of cake.

16 SERVINGS

LEMON GLAZE

> *1 cup powdered sugar*
> *½ teaspoon grated lemon peel*
> *1 teaspoon lemon juice*
> *About 2 tablespoons milk*
> *1 drop yellow food color*

Mix all ingredients until smooth.

Gold and Silver Angel Food Cake with Lemon Glaze

Orange-Lemon Refrigerator Cake

1 cup plus 2 tablespoons all-purpose flour
1 cup granulated sugar
2 teaspoons baking powder
¾ teaspoon salt
½ cup cold water
⅓ cup vegetable oil
3 egg yolks
⅔ cup egg whites (about 6)
½ teaspoon cream of tartar
Orange-Lemon Filling (right)
1 cup whipping cream
¼ cup powdered sugar

Heat oven to 350°. Mix flour, granulated sugar, baking powder and salt. Stir in water, oil and egg yolks until smooth. Beat egg whites and cream of tartar in large bowl until stiff peaks form. Pour egg yolk mixture gradually over egg whites, folding just until mixture is blended. Pour into 2 ungreased round pans, 8 or 9 × 1½ inches.

Bake 25 to 30 minutes or until top springs back when touched lightly in center. Invert pans immediately with edges on 2 other pans until layers are completely cool. Loosen edges from pans with spatula. Turn pans over; hit edges sharply to loosen completely. Remove cake from pans. Prepare Orange-Lemon Filling.

Split layers horizontally into halves. Divide ½ cup filling between layers; frost side and top with remaining filling. Wrap in plastic wrap or aluminum foil and refrigerate at least 12 hours.

Just before serving, beat whipping cream and powdered sugar in chilled bowl until stiff; frost cake. Garnish with grated orange or lemon peel if desired. Refrigerate any remaining cake.

12 TO 16 SERVINGS

ORANGE-LEMON FILLING

½ cup sugar
3 tablespoons cornstarch
⅛ teaspoon salt
1 cup orange juice
½ cup water
2 egg yolks, slightly beaten
2 tablespoons lemon juice
1 tablespoon grated orange peel
1 tablespoon butter or margarine

Mix sugar, cornstarch and salt in 2-quart saucepan. Stir in orange juice and water gradually. Cook over medium heat, stirring constantly, until mixture thickens and boils. Boil and stir 1 minute. Stir at least half of the hot mixture slowly into egg yolks. Blend egg yolk mixture into hot mixture in saucepan. Boil 1 minute, stirring constantly; remove from heat. Stir in lemon juice, orange peel and butter. Refrigerate about 1 hour or until set. Gently stir to soften, if necessary, before using.

Best Chocolate Cake with Fudge Frosting

2 cups all-purpose flour
2 cups sugar
½ cup shortening
¾ cup water
¾ cup buttermilk
1 teaspoon baking soda
1 teaspoon salt
1 teaspoon vanilla
½ teaspoon baking powder
2 eggs
4 ounces unsweetened chocolate,
*   melted and cooled*
Fudge Frosting (right)

Heat oven to 350°. Grease and flour rectangular pan, 13 × 9 × 2 inches, 3 round pans, 8 × 1½ inches, or 2 round pans, 9 × 1½ inches. Beat all ingredients except Fudge Frosting in large bowl on low speed 30 seconds, scraping bowl constantly. Beat on high speed 3 minutes, scraping bowl occasionally. Pour into pans.

Bake rectangular pan 40 to 45 minutes, round pans 30 to 35 minutes or until wooden pick inserted in center comes out clean. Cool rounds 10 minutes; remove from pans. Cool completely. Prepare Fudge Frosting; frost cake. (Fill layers with ⅓ cup frosting; frost side and top with remaining frosting.)

12 TO 16 SERVINGS

FUDGE FROSTING

2 cups sugar
½ cup shortening
3 ounces unsweetened chocolate
⅔ cup milk
½ teaspoon salt
2 teaspoons vanilla

Mix all ingredients except vanilla in 2½-quart saucepan. Heat to rolling boil, stirring occasionally. Boil 1 minute without stirring. Place saucepan in bowl of ice and water. Beat until frosting is smooth and of spreading consistency; stir in vanilla.

Tipsy Squire

Known variously as tipsy pudding, tipsy parson and squire cake, Tipsy Squire is a version of its liquor-soaked British antecedent, trifle. This simple cake is cut in wedges, which are then split and reassembled with Sherry Custard Sauce, whipped cream and toasted almonds. Marsala, rum, cognac or whiskey may be substituted for the sherry in the sauce.

1¼ cups cake flour
1 teaspoon baking powder
3 eggs
1 cup sugar
½ cup warm milk
½ teaspoon vanilla
¼ cup butter or margarine, melted
Sherry Custard Sauce (page 155)
½ cup whipping cream
½ cup slivered almonds, toasted

Heat oven to 350°. Line bottom of square pan, 9 × 9 × 2 inches, with waxed paper. Mix flour and baking powder; reserve. Beat eggs and sugar in large bowl on high speed about 3 minutes or until thick and lemon colored. Beat in milk and vanilla on low speed. Beat in flour mixture; stir in butter carefully. Pour into pan.

Bake about 25 minutes or until wooden pick inserted in center comes out clean. Cool 10 minutes; remove from pan and cool completely. Prepare Sherry Custard Sauce. Beat whipping cream in chilled bowl until stiff. Cut cake into serving pieces; split each piece horizontally into halves. Place bottom half on serving plate; top with 3 tablespoons custard sauce. Cover with other half; top with 2 to 3 tablespoons custard sauce. Garnish with whipped cream and almonds.

9 SERVINGS

Cream Puffs

1 cup water
½ cup butter or margarine
1 cup all-purpose flour
4 eggs
Whipped Cream Fillings (below)
Powdered sugar

Heat oven to 400°. Heat water and butter to rolling boil in 2½-quart saucepan. Stir in flour. Stir vigorously over low heat about 1 minute or until mixture forms a ball; remove from heat. Beat in eggs, all at once; continue beating until smooth. Drop dough by scant ¼ cupfuls about 3 inches apart onto ungreased cookie sheet.

Bake 35 to 40 minutes or until puffed and golden. Cool on wire rack away from draft. Cut off tops; pull out any filaments of soft dough. Fill puffs with one of the Whipped Cream Fillings. Replace tops; dust with powdered sugar. Serve immediately or refrigerate up to 4 hours.

10 TO 12 CREAM PUFFS

WHIPPED CREAM FILLINGS

Sweetened Whipped Cream. Beat 1 cup whipping cream, ¼ cup powdered sugar and ½ teaspoon vanilla in chilled bowl until stiff. Enough filling for 6 puffs.

Tropical Whipped Cream. Beat 1 cup whipping cream, ¼ cup powdered sugar and ½ teaspoon vanilla in chilled bowl until stiff. Fold in ⅓ cup crushed pineapple, well drained, ⅓ cup chopped toasted almonds and ⅓ cup flaked coconut. Enough filling for 10 puffs.

Spiced Whipped Cream. Beat 1 cup whipping cream, ¼ cup powdered sugar, ½ teaspoon ground cinnamon or ground nutmeg or ¼ teaspoon ground ginger and ½ teaspoon vanilla in chilled bowl until stiff. Enough filling for 10 puffs.

Strawberry Shortcake

1 quart strawberries, sliced
1 cup sugar
2 cups all-purpose flour
2 tablespoons sugar
3 teaspoons baking powder
1 teaspoon salt
⅓ cup shortening
1 cup milk
Butter or margarine, softened
Whipping cream or sweetened whipped cream

Sprinkle strawberries with 1 cup sugar; let stand 1 hour. Heat oven to 450°. Grease round pan, 8 × 1½ inches. Mix flour, 2 tablespoons sugar, the baking powder and salt. Cut in shortening until mixture is crumbly. Stir in milk just until blended. Pat dough evenly in pan.

Bake 15 to 20 minutes or until golden brown. Split layer horizontally into halves while hot. Spread with butter; fill and top with strawberries. Serve warm with cream.

6 SERVINGS

Individual Strawberry Shortcakes. Decrease milk to ¾ cup. Smooth dough into ball on lightly floured cloth-covered board. Knead 20 to 25 times. Roll or pat dough with floured hands to ½-inch thickness; cut with floured 3-inch biscuit cutter. Place 1 inch apart on ungreased cookie sheet. Bake 10 to 12 minutes or until golden brown.

6 SHORTCAKES

Chocolate Fudge Sauce

Fudge sauce made at home is so easy. It can dress up desserts of all kinds, but the ideal partner is French Vanilla Ice Cream (page 203).

¾ cup whipping cream
1 cup sugar
2 ounces unsweetened chocolate, chopped
2 tablespoons butter or margarine
½ teaspoon vanilla
¼ teaspoon salt

Heat whipping cream, sugar and chocolate to boiling in 2-quart saucepan over medium heat, stirring constantly. Boil 2 to 3 minutes, stirring occasionally, until slightly thickened and sugar is completely dissolved; remove from heat. Stir in butter, vanilla and salt. Serve warm. Cover and refrigerate no longer than 4 weeks. Heat before serving.

1½ CUPS

Microwave Directions. Mix whipping cream, sugar and chocolate in 4-cup microwavable measure. Microwave uncovered on medium (50%) 5 to 6 minutes, stirring every 2 minutes, to boiling. Boil 6 minutes, stirring every 2 minutes, until slightly thickened and sugar is completely dissolved. Stir in butter, vanilla and salt.

Orange Charlotte Russe

This import from France, already popular almost 200 years ago, molds Bavarian cream in a ladyfinger-lined springform pan. Once unmolded, the cake is freestanding and elegant. The frosted grapes sparkle, adding an eighteenth century note of excess.

1½ cups boiling water
1 package (6 ounces) orange-flavored gelatin
1 tablespoon grated orange peel
1 cup orange juice
1 tablespoon lemon juice
3 egg whites
½ teaspoon cream of tartar
2 cups whipping cream
1½ packages (3-ounce size) ladyfingers
Frosted Grapes (right)

Pour boiling water on gelatin in medium bowl; stir until gelatin is dissolved. Stir in orange peel, orange juice and lemon juice. Place bowl in bowl of ice and water, or refrigerate 20 to 60 minutes, stirring occasionally, until mixture mounds slightly when dropped from a spoon.

Beat egg whites and cream of tartar in large bowl until stiff. Fold gelatin mixture into egg whites. Beat whipping cream in chilled bowl until stiff. Fold whipped cream into egg white mixture.

Cut ladyfingers lengthwise into halves. Line side of ungreased springform pan, 9 × 3 inches, with ladyfingers, cut sides in. Arrange remaining ladyfingers to fill bottom of pan. Pour gelatin mixture into pan; smooth top. Refrigerate about 3 hours or until firm. Loosen from side of pan; remove side of pan. Garnish with Frosted Grapes.

12 SERVINGS

FROSTED GRAPES

1 tablespoon water
1 teaspoon corn syrup
Small clusters of grapes
Granulated sugar

Mix water and corn syrup. Dip grapes into corn syrup mixture; dip into sugar. Place on wire rack to dry.

French Vanilla Ice Cream

Although ice cream has been popular in the United States since Colonial times, neither vanilla nor chocolate was a widely available flavoring at that time. Ice cream sundaes, topped with sauces, syrups, nuts, fruit, marshmallow and mounds of whipped cream, appeared in the 1890s. "French" vanilla ice cream is characterized by a cooked custard base.

½ cup sugar
¼ teaspoon salt
1 cup milk
3 egg yolks, beaten
1 tablespoon vanilla
2 cups whipping cream

Mix sugar, salt, milk and egg yolks in 2-quart saucepan. Heat just to boiling over medium heat, stirring constantly. Pour into bowl. Cover and refrigerate about 2 hours or until cold. Stir in vanilla and whipping cream. Pour into ice-cream freezer. Freeze according to manufacturer's directions.

1 QUART

Fresh Cherry Ice Cream. Decrease vanilla to 1 teaspoon. Stir in 1 cup coarsley chopped pitted dark sweet cherries (about 8 ounces) with the vanilla and whipping cream.

Orange Charlotte Russe

Chapter 12

COOKIES AND SWEETS

This chapter opens with the quintessential American treat: the Chocolate Chip Cookie. Even during times of hardship, when necessities have been scarce—from barren seventeenth-century winters to the terrible war years of this century—we have always found (or improvised) the ingredients needed to bake these sweet little cakes. Here are cookies to answer every wish: easy drop cookies for moist results with little fuss, lovingly cut-out shapes to make a rainy afternoon pass quickly, bar cookies that are quick to mix and bake into "good keepers" that travel well, perfect for lunch boxes, picnics and care packages. The English word cookie comes from the Dutch for "little cake," koekje, and from our colonial days, cookie- and doughnut-cutters have been kitchen essentials.

Sweets are sometimes thought to be for children only, but that wasn't always so. The ice cream socials of the Victorian age were geared to adult tastes in every way, from ice cream flavors to flirting. The taffy pull was another social event, one enjoyed equally by young adults and entire families, from grandparents to little ones. Sweets make lovely, welcome gifts, for holidays and homecomings, birthdays and housewarmings. Some of the candies that follow use the ages-old techniques of testing "soft ball" and "hard crack" stages, made so easy by modern candy thermometers, and some candies require no cooking at all. Reading through Creamy Caramels and Peanut Brittle, Marshmallows and rich Chocolate Fudge, the only difficulty lies in choosing which recipe to make first.

Chocolate Chip Cookies (page 206)

Molasses Crinkles

Molasses was the chief sweetener in American homes in the eighteenth and early nineteenth centuries, so it appears in many traditional cookie recipes. These chewy cookies with crackled sugary tops have long been a favorite after-school treat.

1 cup packed brown sugar
½ cup butter or margarine, softened
¼ cup shortening
¼ cup molasses
1 egg
2 cups all-purpose flour
2 teaspoons baking soda
1 teaspoon ground cinnamon
1 teaspoon ground ginger
½ teaspoon ground cloves
¼ teaspoon salt
Granulated sugar

Mix brown sugar, butter, shortening, molasses and egg. Stir in remaining ingredients except granulated sugar. Cover and refrigerate at least 1 hour but no longer than 24 hours.

Heat oven to 375°. Shape dough into 1¼-inch balls; roll in granulated sugar. Place about 2 inches apart on ungreased cookie sheet. Bake 10 to 11 minutes or just until set. Cool slightly; remove from cookie sheet.

ABOUT 3 DOZEN COOKIES

Peanut Butter Cookies

½ cup granulated sugar
½ cup packed brown sugar
½ cup peanut butter
¼ cup shortening
¼ cup butter or margarine, softened
1 egg
1¼ cups all-purpose flour
¾ teaspoon baking soda
½ teaspoon baking powder
¼ teaspoon salt

Mix sugars, peanut butter, shortening, butter and egg. Stir in remaining ingredients. Cover and refrigerate at least 3 hours but no longer than 24 hours.

Heat oven to 375°. Shape dough into 1¼-inch balls. Place about 3 inches apart on ungreased cookie sheet. Flatten in crisscross pattern with fork dipped into flour or sugar. Bake 9 to 10 minutes or until light brown. Cool slightly; remove from cookie sheet.

ABOUT 3 DOZEN COOKIES

Cherry Blinks

Wheaties® whole wheat flake cereal was introduced in 1924 by General Mills. Two years later, the Wheaties® Quartet performed the first singing commercial. Crushed Wheaties® make a crunchy coating for these fruit-and-nut cookies, invented in 1941.

½ cup sugar
⅓ cup shortening
1 tablespoon plus 1½ teaspoons milk
1 teaspoon vanilla
1 egg
1 cup all-purpose flour
½ teaspoon baking powder
¼ teaspoon baking soda
¼ teaspoon salt
½ cup raisins
½ cup chopped nuts
1¾ cups whole wheat flake cereal, crushed
Candied or maraschino cherries

Heat oven to 375°. Mix sugar, shortening, milk, vanilla and egg. Stir in flour, baking powder, baking soda and salt. Stir in raisins and nuts. Drop dough by teaspoonfuls into crushed wheat flakes; roll gently until completely coated. Place cookies about 2 inches apart on ungreased cookie sheet. Press a cherry into each cookie. Bake until just set, 10 to 12 minutes. Remove from cookie sheet immediately.

ABOUT 3 DOZEN COOKIES

Thumbprint Cookies

¼ cup packed brown sugar
¼ cup shortening
¼ cup butter or margarine, softened
½ teaspoon vanilla
1 egg, separated
1 cup all-purpose flour
¼ teaspoon salt
¾ cup finely chopped nuts
Jelly

Heat oven to 350°. Mix brown sugar, shortening, butter, vanilla and egg yolk. Stir in flour and salt until dough holds together. Shape into 1-inch balls.

Beat egg white slightly. Dip each ball into egg white; roll in nuts. Place about 1 inch apart on ungreased cookie sheet; press thumb deeply into center of each. Bake about 10 minutes or until light brown. Remove from cookie sheet immediately; cool. Fill thumbprints with jelly.

ABOUT 3 DOZEN COOKIES

Cherry Blinks and Thumbprint Cookies

Sour Cream Sugar Cookies

1 cup sugar
½ cup butter or margarine, softened
½ cup sour cream
1½ teaspoons vanilla
1 egg
2½ cups all-purpose flour
1 teaspoon baking powder
½ teaspoon baking soda
½ teaspoon salt
Sugar

Heat oven to 400°. Mix 1 cup sugar, the butter, sour cream, vanilla and egg. Stir in remaining ingredients except sugar. Drop dough by rounded teaspoonfuls into sugar; roll gently until completely coated. Place about 2 inches apart on ungreased cookie sheet. Flatten to about ¼-inch thickness with bottom of glass. Bake 7 to 8 minutes or just until set. Cool slightly; remove from cookie sheet.

ABOUT 4 DOZEN COOKIES

Marguerites

In this turn-of-the-century recipe, a sweet spread of nutty meringue bakes onto saltine crackers, for a unique flavor combination. A Fanny Farmer version, published in 1905, added melted marshmallows to the meringue topping.

1 egg white
¼ cup sugar
¼ teaspoon vanilla
¼ cup chopped nuts
18 saltine crackers

Heat oven to 400°. Beat egg white until foamy. Beat in sugar, 1 tablespoon at a time; continue beating until stiff and glossy. Beat in vanilla. Stir in nuts. Spoon 1 level tablespoon egg white mixture onto each cracker;

spread to edges. Place slightly apart on ungreased cookie sheet. Bake 7 to 9 minutes or until golden brown. Store loosely covered.

1½ dozen cookies

Fudgy Chocolate Brownies

Brownies have been popular since the 1920s, and were originally called "Bangor Brownies" after the city in Maine where they first became popular. Brownie mavens debate: Should these dark bar cookies be dense and chewy like candy or softly textured like cake? Our version makes a large pan of the fudgy variety.

½ cup butter or margarine
1 package (12 ounces) semisweet chocolate chips
1½ cups sugar
1¼ cups all-purpose flour
1 teaspoon vanilla
½ teaspoon baking powder
½ teaspoon salt
3 eggs
1 cup coarsely chopped nuts

Heat oven to 350°. Grease rectangular pan, 13 × 9 × 2 inches. Heat butter and 1 cup of the chocolate chips in 3-quart saucepan over low heat, stirring constantly, until melted. Stir in sugar, flour, vanilla, baking powder, salt and eggs until smooth. Stir in remaining chocolate chips. Spread in pan; sprinkle with nuts. Bake about 30 minutes or until center is set; cool completely. Cut into about 2 × 1½-inch bars. Store tightly covered.

36 BROWNIES

Fudgy Chocolate Brownies

Marshmallows

Homemade marshmallows are melt-in-your-mouth delights! Marshmallows are named for the root of the marshmallow plant *(Althaea officinalis)* used in French recipes from the nineteenth century. By the 1870s, an American invention allowed for less expensive commercial production; the marshmallow grew in popularity. Homemade marshmallows were traditionally enjoyed as dainty confections by themselves and were added to thick, sweet fillings and frostings.

¼ cup cornstarch
¼ cup powdered sugar
2 envelopes unflavored gelatin
½ cup cold water
1 cup granulated sugar
¾ cup light corn syrup
½ cup water
1 egg white
⅛ teaspoon cream of tartar
1 teaspoon vanilla

Mix cornstarch and powdered sugar. Line rectangular pan, 13 × 9 × 2 inches with aluminum foil. Grease foil; coat with cornstarch mixture. Reserve remaining cornstarch mixture.

Sprinkle gelatin on ½ cup cold water in small bowl to soften. Heat granulated sugar, corn syrup and ½ cup water to boiling in 2-quart saucepan, stirring constantly, just until sugar is dissolved. Cook, without stirring, to 250° on candy thermometer or until small amount of mixture dropped into very cold water forms a firm ball that holds its shape but is pliable; remove from heat. Stir in gelatin mixture until gelatin is dissolved.

Beat egg white and cream of tartar in large bowl until stiff peaks form. Continue beating on high speed while adding hot syrup in a thin stream. Add vanilla; beat on high speed until soft peaks form. Pour into pan; spread evenly.

Let stand uncovered at room temperature about 1½ hours or until top is dry. Turn out onto flat surface generously dusted with reserved cornstarch mixture; remove foil. Cut into about 1-inch squares with long knife dipped into cornstarch mixture or with kitchen shears. Roll squares in cornstarch mixture to coat all sides; let stand uncovered on wire rack 1 hour or until dry. Store tightly covered at room temperature up to 2 weeks.

ABOUT **84** MARSHMALLOWS

Spicy Sugared Nuts

1 tablespoon slightly beaten egg white
2 cups pecan or walnut halves
¼ cup sugar
2 teaspoons ground cinnamon
¼ teaspoon ground nutmeg
¼ teaspoon ground cloves

Heat oven to 300°. Mix egg white and pecans until pecans are coated and sticky. Mix remaining ingredients; sprinkle over pecans, stirring until pecans are completely coated. Spread in single layer in ungreased jelly roll pan, 15½ × 10½ × 1 inch. Bake 30 minutes; cool completely.

ABOUT **2** CUPS

Divinity

2²/₃ cups sugar
²/₃ cup light or dark corn syrup
¹/₂ cup water*
2 egg whites
1 teaspoon vanilla
²/₃ cup coarsely chopped nuts

Cook sugar, corn syrup and water in 2-quart saucepan over low heat, stirring constantly, until sugar is dissolved. Cook, without stirring, to 260° on candy thermometer or until small amount of mixture dropped into very cold water forms a hard ball that holds its shape but is pliable.

While mixture boils, beat egg whites in large bowl just until stiff peaks form. Continue beating while adding hot syrup in thin steam. Add vanilla; beat on high speed until mixture holds its shape and becomes slightly dull. (Mixture may become too stiff for mixer.) Fold in nuts. Drop mixture from buttered spoon onto waxed paper. Let stand at room temperature at least 12 hours, turning candies over once, until candies feel firm. Store in airtight container.

ABOUT 48 CANDIES

*Use 1 tablespoon less water on humid days.

Note. For best results, use stand mixer.

Microwave Directions. Mix sugar, corn syrup and water in 8-cup microwavable measure until sugar is thoroughly moistened. Microwave uncovered on high 13 to 15 minutes, stirring once after 5 minutes, to 260° on microwave candy thermometer or until small amount of mixture dropped into very cold water forms a hard ball that holds its shape but is pliable. Continue as directed.

Peanut Brittle

1¹/₂ teaspoons baking soda
1 teaspoon water
1 teaspoon vanilla
1¹/₂ cups sugar
1 cup water
1 cup light or dark corn syrup
3 tablespoons butter or margarine
1 pound shelled unroasted peanuts

Butter 2 cookie sheets, 15¹/₂ × 12 inches; keep warm. Mix baking soda, 1 teaspoon water and the vanilla; reserve. Mix sugar, 1 cup water and the corn syrup in 3-quart saucepan. Cook over medium heat, stirring occasionally, to 240° on candy thermometer or until small amount of mixture dropped into very cold water forms a soft ball that flattens when removed from water.

Stir in butter and peanuts. Cook, stirring constantly, to 300° or until small amount of mixture dropped into very cold water separates into threads that are hard and brittle. (Watch carefully so mixture does not burn.) Remove from heat immediately; stir in reserved baking soda mixture until light and foamy.

Pour half of the candy mixture onto each cookie sheet and quickly spread about ¹/₄ inch thick (syrup will be very hot); cool. Break into pieces.

ABOUT 2 POUNDS CANDY

Microwave Directions. Omit all water. Mix sugar, corn syrup and peanuts in microwavable 8-cup measure. Microwave uncovered on high 10 to 14 minutes, stirring every 5 minutes, until peanuts are light brown. Stir in vanilla and butter until blended. Microwave uncovered 4 to 6 minutes to 300° on microwave candy thermometer or until small amount of mixture dropped into very cold water separates into threads that are hard and brittle. (Watch carefully so mixture does not burn.) Stir in baking soda quickly until light and foamy. Continue as directed.

Chapter 13

CONDIMENTS AND PRESERVES

*O*ur reasons for "putting up" fruits and vegetables are different from those of our grandmothers. Thanks to refrigeration and freezing, it is no longer necessary to rely on canning for preserving foods. And since supermarkets offer plentiful supplies of produce year 'round, there is no need to put away large batches of food for the long winter months.

Nonetheless, it is a great pleasure to make rich-tasting condiments and preserves from scratch, whether for home use or to give away. A homemade jam brightens breakfast, thickly spread on crisp, buttery toast. Jellies and jams are heavenly at tea time, too, or with hot, flaky biscuits at the dinner table. Tangy chutneys and pickles give new excitement to cold roasts and leftovers. There is no more thoughtful hostess gift than a variety of homemade pickles and preserves, packed into pretty jars and decorated with calico and ribbon.

Our small-batch recipes capture the flavor and fun of homemade condiments without the steamy, all-day work of hot water-bath processing. The food processor and the microwave oven speed up production even further. Some of the recipes that follow are for immediate eating, while many can be held for as long as two months.

Watermelon Pickles (page 226), Plum Preserves (page 236) and
Quick Buttermilk Bread (page 143)

Bread-and-Butter Pickles

Like other fresh-pack pickles, these are canned in a spicy vinegar solution. Don't be tempted to skip the standing time in the salted ice water, because that's what gives the pickles their crispness. Using "pickling" (noniodized or kosher) salt keeps the brine from clouding.

*6 cups thinly sliced unpared pickling cucumbers
   (about 2 pounds)*
2 medium onions, thinly sliced
2 tablespoons noniodized or pickling salt
1 cup water
1¼ cups sugar
1¼ cups cider or white vinegar
1 tablespoon mustard seed
½ teaspoon celery seed
½ teaspoon ground turmeric

Mix cucumbers and onions in large glass or plastic bowl. Dissolve salt in water; pour over vegetables. Cover vegetables with layer of ice cubes or crushed ice. Weight with a heavy object and let stand 3 hours.

Drain vegetables thoroughly. Heat sugar, vinegar, mustard seed, celery seed and turmeric to boiling in Dutch oven; add vegetables. Heat to boiling. Immediately pack in hot, sterilized jars, leaving ¼-inch headspace. Wipe rims of jars; seal. Cool on rack 1 hour. Store in refrigerator up to 2 months.

ABOUT 3 PINTS PICKLES

Corn Relish

4 ears fresh corn*
½ cup water
2 tablespoons chopped green bell pepper
1 tablespoon finely chopped onion
1 jar (2 ounces) diced pimiento, drained
½ cup sugar
½ cup cider or white vinegar
½ teaspoon celery seed
¼ teaspoon salt
¼ teaspoon mustard seed
¼ teaspoon red pepper sauce

Cut enough kernels from corn to measure 2 cups. Heat water to boiling in 1½-quart saucepan; add corn. Heat to boiling; reduce heat. Cover and cook over medium heat 9 to 10 minutes or until corn is tender; drain.

Mix corn, bell pepper, onion and pimiento in medium heatproof glass or plastic bowl. Heat sugar, vinegar, celery seed, salt, mustard seed and pepper sauce to boiling; boil 2 minutes. Pour hot liquid over corn mixture. Cover and refrigerate at least 4 hours but no longer than 5 days.

ABOUT 2 CUPS RELISH

*1 can (16 ounces) whole kernel corn, drained, or 2 cups frozen whole kernel corn, thawed, can be substituted for the cooked fresh corn.

Microwave Directions. Place 2 cups corn and 2 tablespoons water in 1½-quart microwavable casserole. Cover tightly and microwave on high 7 to 8 minutes, stirring after 3 minutes, until corn is tender. Add bell pepper, onion and pimiento. Decrease vinegar to ⅓ cup. Mix sugar, vinegar, celery seed, salt, mustard seed and pepper sauce in 4-cup microwavable measure. Microwave uncovered on high 2 to 3 minutes until boiling; stir. Continue as directed.

Pepper Relish

Relishes are condiments made from chopped vegetables or fruits. This recipe can be varied according to the type of peppers used, to produce red or green relish, or a sprightly two-tone combination. Serve the relish with roast meats or spread onto cold meat and cheese sandwiches.

7 cups chopped red or green bell peppers
(about 6 large)
2 red or green jalapeño peppers (with seeds),
finely chopped
1 small onion, chopped
1 tablespoon pickling or noniodized salt
1½ cups sugar
1 cup white vinegar

Mix peppers, onion and salt in large glass or plastic bowl. Cover and refrigerate 12 hours.

Drain peppers and onion, pressing out all liquid. Heat peppers, onion, sugar and vinegar to boiling in 3-quart saucepan, stirring frequently; reduce heat. Simmer uncovered about 45 minutes, stirring frequently, until mixture is thickened. Immediately pack in hot, sterilized jars, leaving ¼-inch headspace. Wipe rims of jars; seal. Cool on rack 1 hour. Store in refrigerator up to 2 months.

ABOUT 4 HALF-PINTS RELISH

Cranberry-Orange Relish

1 package (12 ounces) fresh or frozen cranberries
1 unpeeled orange, cut up
1 cup sugar
1 tablespoon finely chopped crystallized ginger

Grind cranberries and orange pieces in food grinder, using fine blade. Stir in sugar and ginger. Cover and refrigerate at least 24 hours but no longer than 1 week.

ABOUT 2½ CUPS RELISH

Food Processor Directions. Cut orange into about 1-inch pieces. Place cranberries and orange pieces in workbowl fitted with steel blade. Cover and process with short on-and-off motions about 15 seconds or until evenly chopped. Place mixture in bowl; stir in sugar and ginger. Continue as directed.

Pepper Relish

Shaker Peaches

The Shakers prepared their food with the same dedication to quality, functionalism and simplicity that went into their furniture. Here, summer's fragrant peaches are simply transformed into a lightly sweetened condiment for meat and poultry, with just a kiss of rose water. A dollop of lightly whipped cream or vanilla ice cream turns the peaches into dessert.

3 tablespoons butter or margarine
2 tablespoons water
4 large firm ripe peaches, peeled,
  halved and pitted
Rose water
8 teaspoons brown sugar

Heat butter and water in heavy 10-inch skillet until butter is melted. Place peach halves, hollow sides up, in skillet. Place 1 drop rose water and 1 teaspoon brown sugar in each hollow. Cover and simmer about 20 minutes or until peaches are tender. Serve with syrup from skillet.

8 PEACH HALVES

Microwave Directions. Place butter in round microwavable dish, 8 × 1½ inches. Microwave uncovered on high 30 to 45 seconds or until butter is melted. Omit water. Place peach halves, hollow sides up, in dish. Place 1 drop rose water and 1 teaspoon brown sugar in each hollow. Cover tightly and microwave 4 to 6 minutes, rotating dish ¼ turn every 2 minutes, until peaches are tender.

Rhubarb-Strawberry Conserve

A conserve is a spread made with a mixture of large pieces of fruits combined with raisins and nuts. Rhubarb was more popularly enjoyed in years gone by. The bold, fresh flavor of rhubarb has traditionally been tamed and sweetened by strawberry.

2 cups sugar
½ cup water
4 cups 1-inch pieces rhubarb (about 1 pound)
1 pint strawberries, cut into halves
½ cup coarsely chopped walnuts
¼ cup golden raisins

Heat sugar and water to boiling in 3-quart saucepan, stirring constantly; add rhubarb. Boil gently about 15 minutes, stirring frequently, until thick. Stir in strawberries, walnuts and raisins. Heat to boiling; boil gently 5 minutes. Quickly skim off foam. Immediately pour mixture into hot, sterilized jars, leaving ¼-inch headspace. Wipe rims of jars; seal. Cool on rack 1 hour. Store in refrigerator up to 2 months.

ABOUT 4 HALF-PINTS CONSERVE

Chunky Cinnamon Applesauce

*4 medium cooking apples, pared, cored
    and cut into eighths*
½ cup water
½ cup packed brown sugar
¾ teaspoon ground cinnamon
¼ teaspoon ground nutmeg

Heat apples and water to boiling over medium heat; reduce heat. Simmer uncovered 10 to 15 minutes, stirring frequently to break up apples, until tender. Stir in brown sugar, cinnamon and nutmeg. Heat to boiling; boil and stir 1 minute. Serve warm or cold. Cover and refrigerate up to 2 days or freeze up to 2 months.

ABOUT 3 CUPS APPLESAUCE

Microwave Directions. Decrease water to ¼ cup. Place apples and water in 2-quart microwavable casserole. Cover tightly and microwave on high 8 to 10 minutes, stirring after 4 minutes, until apples are tender. Mash apples slightly with fork. Stir in brown sugar, cinnamon and nutmeg. Cover tightly and microwave 2 to 3 minutes or until mixture boils. Continue as directed.

Pear-Apricot Chutney

A chutney is a sweet-and-sour mixture of fruit or vegetables with lively spices. This golden version is equally delicious as a traditional accompaniment to curries and as a luscious filling for cookies, cakes and other sweet dishes. American chutneys, a popular means of "putting by" summer's fresh produce, made great use of the ginger brought to the colonies by eighteenth-century trade ships.

*5 cups coarsely chopped pared pears
    (about 2 pounds)*
3 cups sugar
½ cup snipped dried apricots
1 teaspoon grated lemon peel
*1 teaspoon finely chopped gingerroot or
    ½ teaspoon ground ginger*
3 tablespoons lemon juice

Mix all ingredients in 3-quart saucepan. Heat to boiling over medium heat, stirring frequently. Boil 25 to 30 minutes, stirring occasionally, until mixture thickens. Immediately pour into hot, sterilized jars, leaving ¼-inch headspace. Wipe rims of jars; seal. Cool on rack 1 hour. Store in refrigerator up to 2 months.

ABOUT 4 HALF-PINTS CHUTNEY

CREDITS

PRENTICE HALL PRESS

Vice President and Publisher: Anne M. Zeman
Senior Editor: Rebecca W. Atwater
Editorial Assistant: Rachel Simon
Assistant Art Director: Patricia Fabricant
Photography Designers: Frederick J. Latasa and Angela Carlino
Prop Styling: IDESIGN
Senior Production Manager: Susan Joseph
Production Editor: Philip Metcalf

GENERAL MILLS, INC.

Editor: Karen Couné
Test Kitchen Home Economist: Mary Hallin Johnson
Recipe Copy Editor: Judy Anderson Lund
Editorial Assistant: Phyllis Weinbender
Food Stylists: Cindy Lund, Katie W. McElroy, Mary Sethre
Photographer: Nanci E. Doonan
Photography Assistant: Chuck Carver
Director, Betty Crocker Food and Publications Center: Marcia Copeland
Assistant Manager, Publications: Lois Tlusty